*T*RADITIONAL COUNTRY CRAFTS

TRADITIONAL COUNTRY CRAFTS

MIRANDA INNES

SPECIAL PHOTOGRAPHY BY

LUCY MASON AND CLAY PERRY

conran
OCTOPUS

For Roger and my sons

First published as *The Country Craft Compendium* in 1993
by Conran Octopus Limited
37 Shelton Street, London WC2H 9HN

Reprinted 1998

This paperback edition published in 1997
by Conran Octopus Limited

A catalogue record of this book is available from the British Library
ISBN 1 85029 900 5

Art Director Mary Evans
Art Editor Alison Fenton
Design Assistant and Illustrator Alison Barclay
Project Editor Louise Simpson
Copy Editor Kate Bell
Editorial Assistant Jane Chapman
Picture Research Julia Pashley
Production Controller Sonya Sibbons
Chart Illustrator Frue Bucknall
Rubber stamp for the endpapers
designed by George Thomson
Indexer Hilary Bird

Typeset by Servis Filmsetting Limited, Manchester
Colour separations by Scantrans Pte Limited, Singapore
Printed in China

CONTENTS

INTRODUCTION

Below Rob Shepherd's portfolio in strong, shell-printed linen is a perfect example of the point of crafts – the combination of love and handworked skill that triumphs over the utilitarian and machine-made.

Right A small cabinet is transformed with muted shades of green and ochre and adorned with a flock of swans. *Far right* A miscellany of Andrea Maflin's script and découpage objects, all concocted from tea-stained paper and photocopied documents and etchings. Boxes, clocks, screens and lampshades – the possibilities are as varied as ingenuity allows.

There are few happier ways of passing time than by making something of your own. Crafts are a means of escaping the fuss of life, and all the little decisions – between red stitching or blue, this feather or that shell, a portly pig motif or a copperplate swash capital – serve in some humble way to confirm who you are. There is something tremendously calming about making things. Even the accompanying clutter of tools and pens and paint is seductive, and apt to make your fingers itch with an urge to experiment. Don't resist! Even if your nearest and dearest are puzzled by your new-found fascination with pebbles, or embarrassed by your sudden need to forage for old clothes in junk shops, they will probably come round to appreciate and cherish the finished production in time.

Another important aspect of crafts is fun. There are times when the newspapers are burdened with such gloom, that to keep sane it is necessary to take refuge in a bit of escapism. Crafts, in an innocent and productive way, can provide just that. In childhood, they are indistinguishable from play. The solemn patting of the clay into ponderous containers, or the total concentration required to pin bottle-top wheels to a cardboard box bus, are drawn from the wellsprings of both craft and play. The smaller the child, the more confident he or she is about what should go where and what colour it should be, and where it should finally be displayed.

Probate
POST OFFICE
TELEGRAM

Above *A collection of classic baskets – light, durable and adaptable. Their construction may have changed little over the centuries, but they are still the most attractive containers for household bits and pieces.*

Time and age confuse us as to what we like, whilst too much knowledge insists that we devalue our own creations: in a world that contains the Sistine Chapel ceiling, who needs my quilted pot-holder? This is something to challenge because making things, whatever they are, gladdens the heart. The more you do, the more decisive and skilled you become, the more you should shout about it. Look about you – other people can make the most hideous things and yet be deeply, irritatingly complacent about them.

None of the projects described here are difficult and you should be able to finish most of them in a day. Most can be made with quite ordinary tools and the use of the kitchen table, but you might well find that you want a quiet corner of your home all to yourself where you can keep your tools unmolested by family borrowers and leave your work out undisturbed by mealtimes and children's homework.

Thought for presentation is almost as important as the work itself; a collection of bus tickets can look pretty special if it is framed and mounted with respect, and the Bayeux Tapestry could look like a load of dirty washing if it were scrumpled up in a corner. Ideally, try to display like with like – a wall full of framed samplers has much more impact than one or two – and try to keep to a common denominator of colour. Hot, intense Indian colours work well together, as do cool, Scandinavian bleached blues and greys. Having spent time creating your craftwork, show it off to its best advantage.

I hope that the ideas in this book will get you going, and having tried out the

versions we have explained, you will want to explore museums and study magazines for further inspiration. Many of the craftspeople introduced here have pin-boards for sticking up ideas, postcards, drawings and scraps of fabric. It is also useful to keep a scrapbook of reference pictures, catalogues, sketches, photos, and other inspiring sources.

Once you discover the joys of making things, you will find the world a richer place: there are societies to join, specialist books to read, exhibitions to visit and people to meet who share your interest. Some crafts, especially the more traditional ones, offer a shortcut to E. M. Forster's nostrum: 'Only connect.' No woodworker need ever walk alone; there is an international sorority of quilt-makers ready to welcome any stranger bearing an Olfa cutter; sampler stitchers and rag-rug prodders are only too willing to share their expertise.

All the contributors to this book were happy to explain and demonstrate their individual crafts in this spirit of generosity. Bear in mind, however, that the projects in this book are only suggestions for one possible approach – there are no rigid rules, and there is no cast-iron recipe. The world is there for you to explore and use, and these ideas are presented as a spring-board for your imagination. Most of the projects cost almost nothing to make, so if you don't get it right first time, try again. The important point is to enjoy the process. Many of the people in this book started off by making things as a sideline, just for fun, in relaxing contrast to their real careers. So, clear a space, get out your paints and your sketch-book, and prepare to enjoy yourself.

Above *A diminutive Amish quilt, bringing warmth and comfort to a discreetly expressionless rag doll couple. Having experimented on miniature bedding, you might feel emboldened to make something rather more sizeable to grace your own bed.*

*N*EEDLECRAFT

Ever since primitive man first began to fasten his animal skins together using sinew and a bone needle, people have been stitching. Although the original motive was simply protection against the cold, man's unquenchable passion to decorate soon took over. Whether in the form of the obligatory cross-stitch sampler, the prince's or pauper's patchwork, or the defiantly thrifty rag rug, people learnt how to bring warmth and colour into their lives using simple tools and humble materials.

Above *An 1802 alphabet sampler, whose soft and faded colours are a model of good taste.*
Right *Emma Tennant's cockerel strutting through the stubble – a masterpiece of uninhibited confidence.*

*A*MISH AND *M*ENNONITE *Q*UILTS

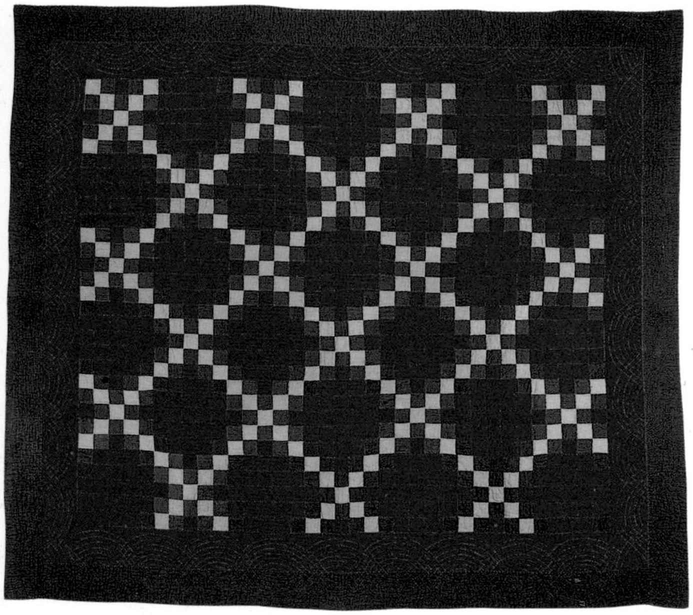

Above *A sizzling example of Mennonite colour in a double Irish chain quilt from Lebanon County, Pennsylvania, made in 1900. The stray cobalt corner may serve as conscious reminder that man is fallible, and only God can create absolute perfection.*

Right *Psychedelic Amish bars, beautifully quilted with floral and princess feather borders.*

Quilts padded with wool, cotton, silk or even paper have a long and honourable history. Beautifully stitched whole-cloth quilts were pre-eminent in the North of England in the last century. Elsewhere, from Canada to Kyoto, patchwork quilts were the thrifty and decorative answer to long hard winters before the advent of central heating. People the world over used whatever they had to hand: in Australia, during the Depression, suiting samples were transformed into rough but comforting wagga rugs, and in Pakistan the old cotton quilt became the filling for the new, hidden by more bright patches of highly symbolic colour. In America, quilts became a national passion pursued with religious zeal by everyone, from society hostesses to the brave and penniless cornland pioneers who lived in troglodyte hardship in Texas at the beginning of this century. There is a bucolic poetry in the names of American quilts: flying geese, windmill blades, bear's paw, tree of life, grandmother's flower garden, sunshine and shadow, barn raising, log cabin. They all refer to a time of slow change and certainties, family ties, a bond of religion, the endless cycle of nature.

In contrast to the copious and charming dimity-print designs which swept America in the nineteenth century, the work of the Anabaptist Amish and Swiss Mennonites stands out as revolutionary. Their quilts use strong plain colours in striking and singular combinations, often given further brilliance by the sober counterpoint of black or dark blue as a background. Simplicity and plainness are the watchwords of

Above Cotton satin, brightly contrasted and heavily quilted in the north bedroom of the Sheldon-Hawks House, Deerfield, Massachusetts.

these profoundly religious sects, and they eschew the frivolity of print, unless it is discreetly relegated to the back of a quilt, unseen by all but the user.

The patches are almost always basic squares and triangles, and are easy to piece together by machine. The favourite and recurring designs are Joseph's coat in rainbow colours; variations on log cabin and Irish chain; nine-patch; bars (which have a passing similarity to British strippy quilts); sunshine and shadow, and the utterly straightforward centre diamond. Usually the design is framed with wide borders. Neither Amish nor Mennonites use appliqué, and though their designs are extremely simple, they have an extraordinary sophistication that makes them true classics. They dyed much of their own wool and cotton, and in their frugal way, used up the good parts of old clothes and sewing scraps to make their quilts, so that while the background may appear to be an even black, on close inspection shade variations are discernible.

The intricacy of the quilting itself often makes up for the plainness of the piecing, with stars, wreaths, curvaceous princess feathers, pineapples and tulips picked out in fine stitching. These days, time-honoured expertise and panache still guide needle and scissors, but the finished product is often marred by the use of synthetic outer fabrics or filling. Raw wool and cotton have been replaced by the convenience of terylene wadding, which does not have sufficient weight or substance to hang well. The kind of padding used imparts its character subtly but noticeably to the finished quilt; it is far better, and probably much cheaper to use an old blanket which will drape in the proper heavy folds than synthetic fillings.

The appeal of Amish and Mennonite quilts lies in their refined needlecraft and their startling originality, which prefigures the work of the modern abstract painters. But the soul of such work is well defined by Horatio Greenough in his journal, *The Travels, Observations, and Experiences of a Yankee Stonecutter*: 'The redundant must be pared down, the superfluous dropped, the necessary itself reduced to its simplest expression, and then we shall find, whatever the organization may be, that beauty was waiting for us.'

Below *A diagonal nine-patch quilt in a striking combination of sombre and bright colours, both design and colours typical of Amish handiwork. Fine quilting loses nothing from the thinness of the interlining – these quilts were neither heavy nor thick.*

Amish Doll's Quilt

Far left *In a haven of quilts, glowing like the rose window of Chartres Cathedral, a young Amish seamstress plies her antiquated treadle machine to create our doll's quilt. Besides the magnificent star quilt, rich colours resplendent against their flattering background of black, there are double wedding rings, log cabin variants and Roman stripes in glorious profusion.* Left *Black is the best foil to bright colours, and is a traditional element in Amish quilts. Here, the simple patchwork designs are embellished with fine and intricate hand-quilting, often stitched in black or navy.*

The Amish don't like to be photographed, let alone photographed and named. The reason for this is the same as their reluctance to allow their children any but the most rudimentary of dolls: a horror of worshipping graven images. They revere simplicity, and never possess televisions or radios.

The original of this tiny doll's quilt was made in around 1938 by the mother of Mrs Miller who runs the Amish store, Miller's Dry Goods. In itself it was an unusual piece of frivolity, since Amish children have been known to be given a stick and a handkerchief in lieu of doll and quilt, and it was also unusual because it was machine quilted. Mrs Miller's daughter now makes reproductions to sell in the shop and at a local gallery run by Stanley Kaufman, who is painstakingly documenting the local Amish and Mennonite legacy of textiles and architecture.

Amish quilts are legendary. At their brilliant best they are composed of simple geometric patterns in sombre resonant colours, electrified with a dazzling charge of brilliant red or blue. The Swartzentruber group of Ohio have remained loyal to the original dark colours and black but most Amish quilters strayed into the use of plain lighter colours in the 1920s.

At Miller's Dry Goods it is estimated that 25 per cent of the quilts sold are traditional Amish, in plain dark colours; 65 per cent are 'country look' – faded blue and pink printed calico; and the remainder are plain wholecloth quilts stitched with traditional and contemporary designs. Nineteenth- and early twentieth-century quilts tended to be much thinner than the present-day predilection for Dacron wadding allows, lined only with thin cotton batting.

The diagonal nine-patch block quilt shown here is typical of Ohio Amish. The broad outer and narrow inner borders are a reminiscence of the original woven coverlets used in Germany. If your heart yearns for something a little larger, it is easy to extrapolate from this tiny example. It is also worth bearing in mind that natural wadding of cotton or wool can replace the Dacron to give a quilt a much more sumptuous drape.

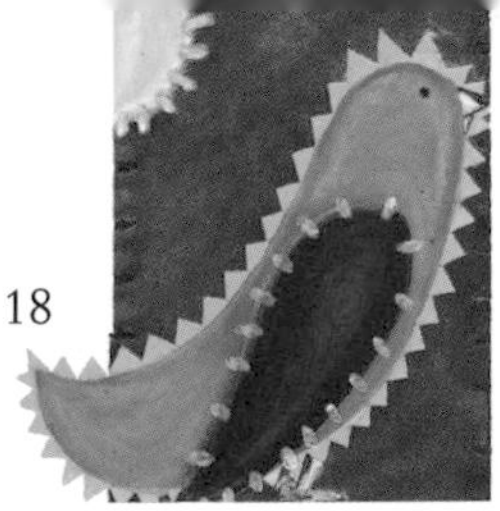

Left The diagonal nine-patch design is traditional and can be enlarged to make a full-size quilt.

Above A diagram to show the correct position of the quilting lines.

PROJECT: *AMISH DOLL'S QUILT*

The strong, plain design and bold colour sense characteristic of the Amish, miniaturized into a whimsical doll's quilt.

To make a 44×35 cm (17½×14 in) Amish doll's quilt you will need:

Materials

- 11 cm (⅛ yd) light blue cotton 92 cm (36 in) wide
- 45 cm (½ yd) cinnamon cotton 92 cm (36 in) wide
- 45 cm (½ yd) navy blue cotton 92 cm (36 in) wide
- 45 cm (½ yd) light Dacron batting (wadding), or flannel to be more authentic
- Needle and white thread for quilting
- Sewing cotton

Tools

- Scissors
- Cardboard template 3 cm (1¼ in) square to make 2 cm (¾ in) square when sewn
- Water-erasable pencil for tracing on to fabric, or sharpened soap to be more authentic
- Ruler
- Sewing machine
- Quilting hoop

1 Mark small nine-patch squares with the cardboard template and water-erasable pencil. Larger squares are 7 cm (2¾ in) when cut and 5.5 cm (2¼ in) when sewn with 6 mm (¼ in) turnings.

2 Piece by machine, working 6 nine-patch squares in strips of 3 and joining them together, then alternating them with plain blocks. Press at every stage. Cut 4 cm (1½ in) wide blue inner border long enough to frame the nine-patch squares. Attach shorter sides first and trim the excess pieced fabric from the back. Cut out and sew 6 cm (2½ in) wide cinnamon border around the blue one, attaching short ends first.

3 Mark quilting lines with a ruler and water-erasable pen. Refer to diagram.

4 Make a sandwich of top, batting and navy blue underside. Tack to hold the layers in place.

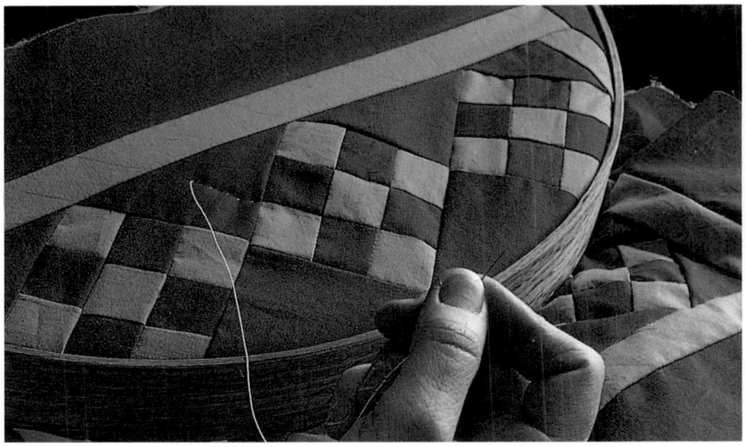

5 Using a quilting hoop, carefully handstitch along all of the quilting lines to the edge, using white thread. Neatly trim around the edges.

6 Stitch 2 cm (1½ in) wide light blue binding to sides. Turn and blind stitch to back. Repeat for top and bottom, finishing the corners neatly.

*T*RADITIONAL SAMPLERS

Above A trio of naïve and charming antique samplers, proving that you do not have to labour for long to produce a worthy commemoration of some major family event. A wedding, A birth, or even a change of address can all be immortalized in a few hours. Far right Samplers add a certain old-fashioned charm to an interior. Plainly framed and boldly grouped they bring a sense of history to a simply furnished room.

The word sampler (also commonly known as sam cloth) comes from the Latin, *exemplar*, meaning an example to be copied. Samplers were probably first made in Italy or Germany towards the end of the fifteenth century, and were used as patterns for household embroidery, clothing and shawl borders. At the time there was no other way to pass on such information, since books had not yet been invented. Eventually, the Dutch became the most enthusiastic sampler-makers, producing acres of cross-stitch tulips, windmills and furniture. The Spanish embroidered samplers of an unusual richness, exploiting the expertise with dye recipes learned from forays to South America and the richness of stylized and geometric design brought to them by the Moors. Their work is resplendent with rich red from cochineal, black and blue from logwood, and yellow and red from safflower.

The oldest surviving British sampler is dated 1598, and was worked by Jane Bostocke to record the birth of Alice Lee on a Tuesday afternoon two years earlier. It is a bold and splendid piece of work, full of roaring bears and cavorting dogs, including a terrier named Juno. She used silk, silver-gilt and gilt thread, and her sophisticated stitches include Algerian eye stitch, buttonhole stitch, ladder stitch, Italian stitch, couching, speckling and French knots. Three samplers are known to have been brought to America from England, and were thus the grandparents of all that followed. The first is dated 1628 and was worked by Anne, the wife of Governor Endicott in Salem; the next was made by Laura Standish before 1655 and bears an improving prayer, and the third was by Abigail Fleetwood to celebrate her marriage to Miles in 1654.

Originally, all samplers served some didactic purpose, whether it were to instil the fear of God, promote acquaintance with the countries of Europe, teach children their letters or simply to pass on to the novice needlewoman the essential skills required to make respectable clothing and household linens. There were exceptions to the general rule of self-improvement through stitchery, however, as samplers came to be worked to celebrate significant family events or to be given as special gifts – from relatives to new-born babies, and from a fiancée to her betrothed: the latter derived from a sixteenth-century European tradition.

In the seventeenth and eighteenth centuries, no self-respecting young woman was without at least one skilled memorial to hours of fine cross-stitch, drawn thread work, embroidered flora and fauna and minutely sewn improving verse taken from such publications as Dr Isaac Watts' *Divine and Moral Songs for Children*. Small girls were apt to be set to work on a text such as:

'Our days, alas! our mortal days
Are short and wretched, too.
Evil and few the patriarch says,
And well the patriarch knew.'

Samplers were included in the school curriculum and as a result lost some of their wayward originality. The usual shape changed from long and narrow to square. Whitework, with white embroidery on a white fabric, was all the rage at this time. Silk, wool and linen thread were used, with the rare extravagance of silver thread. Very occasionally, human hair was incorporated in a design, usually as a memorial. Until chemical dyes became common in the middle of the nineteenth century, most dyes were home-made, from such plant materials as madder, indigo, goldenrod, dock, hickory, peach, hemlock, sumac, sassafras and black walnut, with a splash or two of cochineal, soot, galls and iron buff to add variety.

Far left *Samplers were originally stitched to reinforce moral and religious codes, and to teach small children their alphabets. Reminders of lessons first learnt and a mother's helping hand, they quickly became symbols of patience and innocence.*

Above *The happiest home for a sampler, bringing colour and a touch of human warmth to unpretentious antiques and bare tongued-and-grooved walls.*

With the advent of pattern books such as George Fisher's 1748 *The Instructor: or Young Man's Best Companion*, which included an alphabet for the use of young women, samplers tended to become more utilitarian, recording orderly alphabet letters, as a harbinger of a lifetime marking household linen. For most children this task was penitential, and if their spirit was still unbroken by hours of fine stitching, there was always the ultimate in stultifying boredom – the darning sampler, consisting of a square of linen or wool cut with holes which were then minutely darned in matching or contrasting thread. A necessary skill maybe, but one which might have been better learned on the job. It was a dubious achievement, which was perfected by the Dutch, who took immense pride in darning a sampler so neatly that the front was indistinguishable from the back.

Much more appealing, and with their predictable mastery of design and simplicity, are the Shaker, Amish and Pennsylvania Dutch samplers of the nineteenth century. These are not so much virtuoso exercises in patience, but more of a celebration of the ordinary pleasures of the natural world so venerated by these North American religious communities. There is a very immediate joy in the bright many-windowed square house surrounded with flowers and trees made by an anonymous Pennsylvania Dutch lady; there is a quiet pleasure in the brisk alphabet worked by the Shaker Betsy Crosman in indigo wool on homespun linen; and the ten-year-old Amish girl, Susan Esh, compressed so many of the good things of life into her 1890 wool sampler.

*J*OANNE *H*ARVEY'S *T*RADITIONAL *A*MERICAN *S*AMPLER

Joanne Harvey's interest in samplers grew from a love of needlework that she has suffered from the age of four. 'I just do it morning, noon and night. It's been my whole life, but business-wise it started in 1976. When the children came along, I was at home and I started this out of frustration. The reproduction work that was available at the time just didn't look authentic.'

Joanne started out as an art teacher, before spending many years working at the Henry Ford Museum, where she also met her husband. She now runs a business, 'The Examplarery', which stocks everything an aspiring sampler fanatic might need. She also supplies museums with fastidiously authentic reproduction kits for the classic American samplers, from the very earliest by Loara Standish, dating from 1640 and very complicated, to the cheeringly simple effort worked by Polly Remington, 150 years later. She is a stickler for quality and authenticity, and does not normally supply graphs: 'If you do that, people could change the colour and use the wrong cloth. I just can't do it. Perhaps this is due to my museum training.' You have been warned. She also weaves and spins: 'You understand a lot about antiques that way. You've got to get to the back of the sampler – that's where the story is. That's where you can see how the stitches were done, and the colour is quite different.' She has become something of a sampler historian, and acquired America's second oldest known sampler – the Mary Attwood – quite by chance, guided by a feeling in her bones. She just took one look and knew it was early 1650s, which turned out, after employing the expertise of a genealogist, to be true.

She is at present researching seventeenth-century American samplers, only a handful of which remain today. This involves delving into the niceties of export laws of the time, tracking down the trade routes, reading endless inventories and probate wills, and discovering the state of girls' education. 'Textiles are an afterthought with a lot of museums. They don't hold them in esteem like jewels. And of course, they're just seen as women's work.' She could almost open a museum herself, since she has amassed over 1,200 books on the subject, together with a fair collection of antique sewing tools.

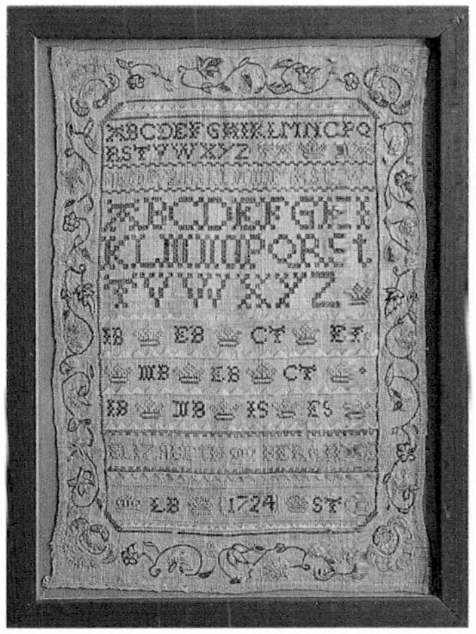

Above *Joanne Harvey in the throes of passionate cross-stitch, with part of her collection of antique sewing paraphernalia to hand.*

Right *An American sampler thought to have originated in Connecticut, with a double border of tulips.* Left *A fairly plain sampler with a scattering of initials, dated 1724.*

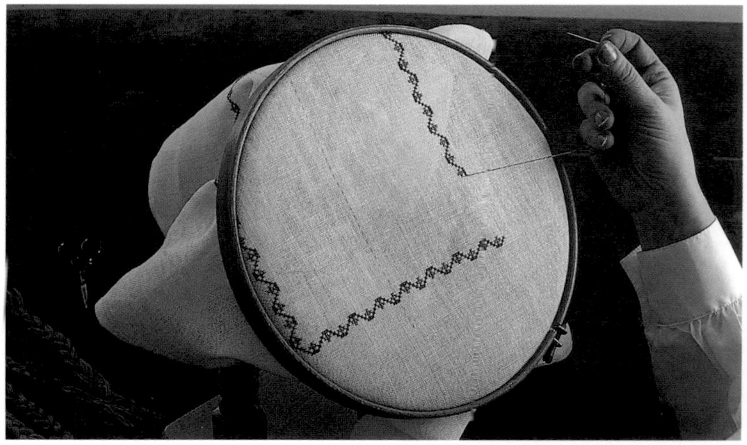

1 Turn under 6 mm (1/4 in) edges of linen and tack. Fold linen exactly in half, then into quarters. Do not iron. Use a contrast running stitch to mark fold lines. Following the chart, begin working on the border at the upper centre, 4.5 cm (1 3/4 in) from the edge of linen. Using green, work entire border following chart. Work flower shapes in gold around border.

2 Work down the sampler following the chart, working left to right. For the fourth inner border, start with green worked across entire piece, followed by gold, grey, toast and blue.

To work your name, count the number of available threads between seventh inner border and outer border design across and down, copy letters on to chart, and work name using blue embroidery cotton.

PROJECT: JOANNE HARVEY'S TRADITIONAL AMERICAN SAMPLER

The poignant legacy of Ann Stevens, aged 8, complete with all her mistakes – leaves a cross-stitched 200-year-old alphabet to adorn your walls. To make Joanne Harvey's traditional American sampler you will need:

Materials

- 27.5×33.5 cm (11×13½ in) piece of cream linen with a 27 thread count
- One skein of DMC embroidery cotton in each of the following colours: Green No. 3051, Blue No. 931, Gold No. 832, Grey No. 646, Toast No. 420

Tools

- Needle and sewing cotton
- Blunt No. 26 tapestry needle
- 17.5 cm (7 in) embroidery hoop
- Embroidery scissors

Instructions for Chart

To work the sampler, use embroidery cotton in 45 cm (18 in) lengths maximum, separated into 2 strands. Work in cross-stitch, counting 2 threads down and 2 threads across for each stitch. Work each stitch from upper left to lower right, then upper right to lower left, completing each stitch as you go and working each stitch into the hole of a previous stitch. Do not pull tight. Never knot the cotton – to begin your first stitch in a new area leave a long thread on front of work and complete a few stitches, pull thread through from front to back and weave it in and out of the backs of these stitches. Subsequently begin and end new threads by working them under a few stitches.

RAG RUGS

Above *Astrology underfoot: a hooked rag rug by J. Stuart Anderson, resplendent with the phases of the moon and the signs of the zodiac.*
Far right *A spare colonial interior, whose tranquil, if somewhat Spartan simplicity is brightened by a chunk of sunshine and an oval plaited and coiled rag rug in different shades of baked earth.*

Rag rugs come from a thrifty school of thought that wastes nothing. No scrap of fabric is thrown away, everything is recycled – cottons in patchwork and wool in the form of rugs. Rag rugs were a comforting fact of life in the years following the Depression and among nineteenth-century country communities, achieving classic status among the Shakers and in the North of England.

There are several methods of construction, the calm, muted tones of braiding in round or oval rugs were characteristic of the Shakers, while the Amish favoured knotting (a technique similar to crochet). Neither method required a backing cloth, whereas hessian or burlap feed sacks were an essential component of the riotously bright hooked or prodded rugs made among farming communities in the North of England, Scandinavia and America. In general, unless trimmed, hooked rugs have a surface, back and front, of loops of continuous fabric, while prodded rugs have a looped backing, with the shaggy raw edges of the short strips on the top. The Egyptians and Copts used similar methods from the third century onwards.

The procedure began with the feed sack, meal- or sugar-bag, which would be unpicked and washed. The design was then drawn with charcoal, taking inspiration from animals, flowers, fruit, patriotic or biblical themes. Those lucky enough to live near the sea added boats, shells, anchors and compasses to the repertoire. Inspiration was also drawn from wallpaper designs, carved furniture, oriental rugs and porcelain. Where imagination failed utterly, occasional rugs remain proclaiming the original message on the feed sack in fine multi-coloured loops. 'Home Sweet Home' was a favourite inscription, and 'Welcome', 'Good Luck' and 'Call Again' frequently

appeared underfoot. Many late nineteenth-century American rugs originated from an entrepreneurial tin peddlar, Edward Sands Frost, who cut stencils from his tin for rugmakers to use as templates.

'Did I go to Boston to get my stencils made? Oh no, I went out to the stable where I had some old iron and some old wash boilers I had bought for their copper bottoms, took the old tin off them and made my first stencil out of it. I forged my tools to cut the stencils with. I made a cutting block out of old lead and zinc.

'I began making small stencils of single flowers, scrolls, leaves, buds, etc. Then I could with a stencil brush print in ink in plain figures much faster than I could sketch. Thus I reduced ten hours' labor to two and a half hours. I began to print patterns and put them in my peddler's cart and offer them for sale. The news of my invention of stamped rugs spread like magic – I became known as Frost the rug man.'

Above *Stacked and stitched, felted wool medallions in an unusual bedroom rug, with an elaborate fishscale border. The quiet, sludgy Shaker green repeats in floor and furniture to epitomize a classic American style that is both spare and comfortable.*

Wool was the most durable fabric, and still has a magical capacity to repel dirt – for this reason old tweed skirts and felted jerseys are eagerly snapped up at car-boot sales by rag rug makers. Synthetic and man-made fabrics are to be avoided where possible.

After the preparation of the backing, the next stage in the production line consisted of one of the smaller members of the family sitting on top of a pile of rags, and assiduously tearing or cutting them into long narrow strips. These were then sewn together, and wound into large balls ready to use for hooked rugs. Prodded rugs were made with short strips about 10 cm×4 cm (4×1½ in). The colours of the finished rugs reflected the fashionable clothing of the time – in the late nineteenth century these tended to be red (from flannel underwear), black and purple, but natural dyes were used to add variety, ranging from brick dust to berries and black walnut skins. Light and age have faded some colours while others remain as clear as ever – this mutability contributes to the charm of old rugs, and close, uneven shades of different colours give an air of antique richness.

Speedy workers could hook two rugs each winter. A gaggle of ladies could complete a rug quite quickly at a rug-hooking bee, and repetitive geometric motifs were the obvious choice of design to be worked by many hands. The closer and slower the work, the more durable the rug, and uncut loops lasted much longer than sheared raw edges. However, a sculpted pile was the distinctive decorative feature of the rugs from Waldoboro, Maine, which has given its name to any rag rug with a high sheared pile. To preserve rugs as long as possible, housewives kept them face down for most of the time, and hastily turned them over on hearing footsteps up the front path. Not all were precious objects of beauty – there was a tradition in England for random utilitarian rugs which were quickly worked and cheered the hearthside for a time, quietly attracting a season's dust and dirt, after which they became a valuable part of the compost heap. This may be taking recycling a little too far.

Below Strong colours, in distant emulation of geometric Persian rug motifs, enlivened here by a meandering floral border.

Left Now residing safely under lock and key in the Shelburne Museum, the best wildcat in the business has a magnificent expression of rage, and was painstakingly and finely hooked from very slightly varying shades of few colours. The lively unevenness makes an interesting contrast with the flat colour used in the 'Persian' rug.

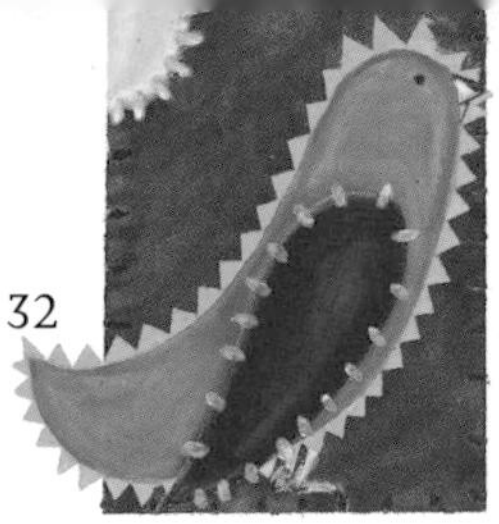

*E*MMA *T*ENNANT'S *R*OOSTER *R*UG

Right Rooster and chicken strut amid a swirling sky. Tweeds and many shades of blue give a lively texture to the rug.
Far left Emma at work, taking advantage of the clear spring light of the Cheviot Hills.
Left Inspirational fragments: sketchbooks with a collection of postcards, drawings, working graphs and colour notes, laid on the hessian backing for our farmyard rug.

Emma Tennant did not set out to become the rag-rug lady. She only embarked on her first rug in order to show a friend that the art was not dead, but alive and well and easy enough for a complete amateur. Initially, it was Winifred Nicholson's rugs that inspired her, along with the feeling that this fine traditional craft had suffered undue neglect. She became hooked – to perpetrate a pun that must have become a weary platitude in the Tennant household. She learned a great deal from her first project: 'It was a cow, and much too big. It took almost a whole winter, and I ended up rather hating it. It's like knitting, it starts off all humps and bumps and hills and hollows, and then, without your being aware of it, you find you're doing it very smoothly.' Whatever Emma's feelings, everybody else admired her cow, so she tackled another rug the next winter: 'It's a winter thing – it's not nice to handle wool in hot weather. The action is warming too; I often work in a room that's too cold to sit in, and feel quite warm – you have to use force to make the loops.'

In her experience, woollen fabrics are the best to use. Anything with a synthetic content attracts dirt, as does cotton, but wool has a satisfactory bounce to it and seems to shrug off the usual household detritus. For the same reason she does not back her rugs, and when they do need cleaning, she hangs them from the washing line and bashes them with a tennis racquet. For an occasional serious clean, she uses a nailbrush and carpet shampoo, but cautions to wait until high summer for this when the rug can dry in the sun.

As people started to hear about her pastime, Emma was inundated with old clothes – dressmakers' scraps, blankets, worsted, tweed, knitted woollens – all of which are grist to her scissors. Double knitting is too thick to use, but men's clothing tends to rug well. She starts off by putting everything in the washing machine: 'It's all the better if it felts or shrinks.' She then cuts the fabric into strips, which she then ties into bundles according to colour: 'Sometimes I start with the fabric and sometimes with a picture. If I'm doing a pig, then I start by looking for a pink blanket; the delphiniums started from a bag of vibrant blues. Dingy tweeds suggest dry stone walls. If the fabrics look pretty all jumbled up in a basket, you will normally find they'll look pretty as a rug.'

Traditionally, there was a great ritual as the new rug was put down in front of the fireplace in the main living room. Last year's went into the kitchen, the one from the year before went to the back door, and the dog's basket was the final resting place of the previous rug.

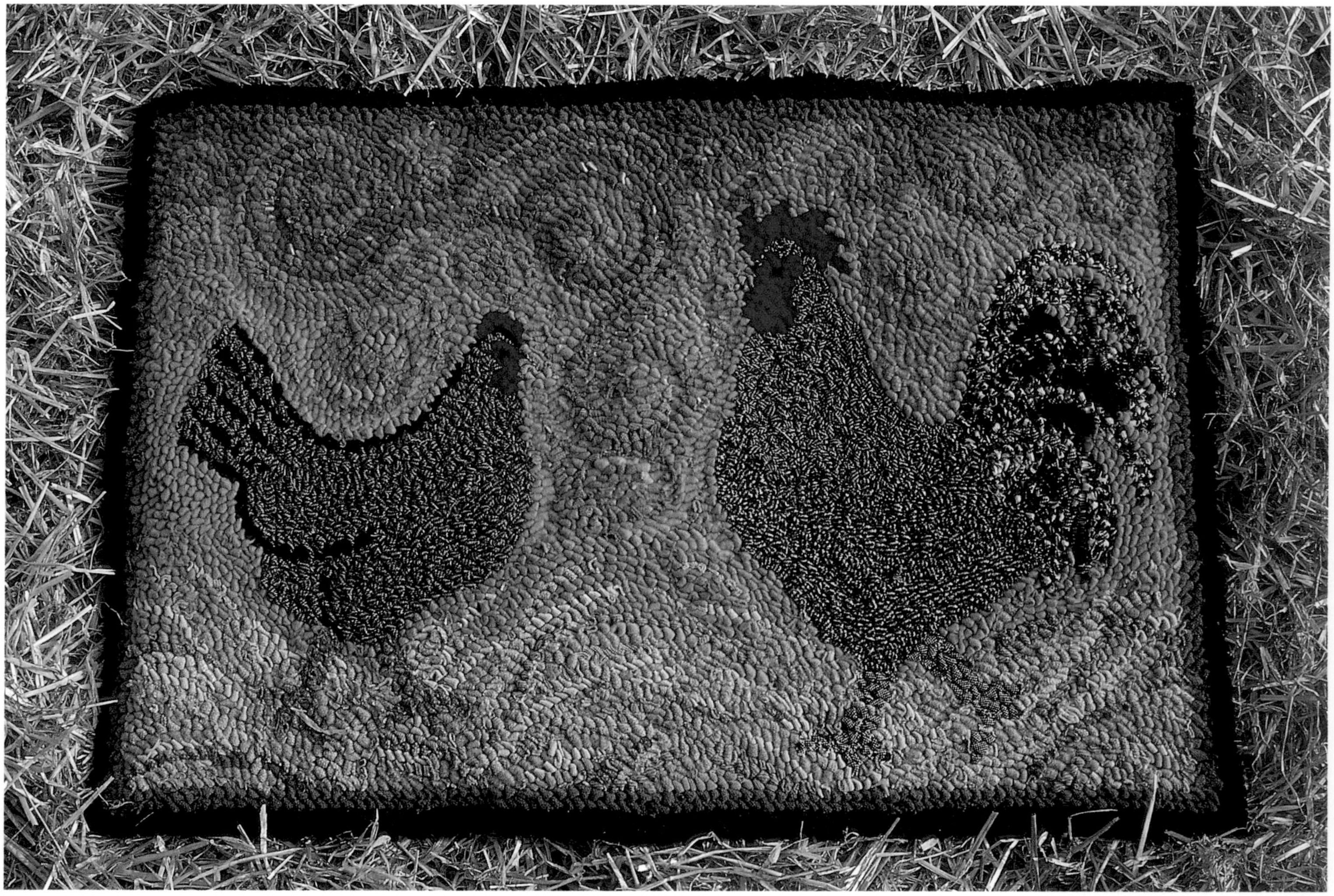

PROJECT: *EMMA TENNANT'S ROOSTER RUG*

A handsome high-stepping cockerel and chicken, produced by magic sleight of hand from nothing more auspicious than a pile of old, felted and colourful woollens. To make Emma's chicken couple you will need:

Materials

- Hessian for the base, measuring the size of the finished rug plus a 3.5 cm (1½ in) hem allowance
- Webbing twice as long as the frame
- Washed woollen rags, cut into 2 cm (¾ in) wide strips, the longer the better, and bundled in colours. Too much contrasting colour gives a jumpy effect. Many subtle shades of a single colour work well.

Tools

- Rug hook (these used to be made from old screwdrivers or gimlets)
- Substantial frame (see *Directory of Craftspeople* page 188)
- Sharp scissors
- Ruler
- Marker pens
- Hammer and tin tacks
- Extra strong button thread

1 Select a simple image from your surroundings, or use a photograph as a basis for your design. To transfer your design to the hessian, you can either make a template or square up the design.

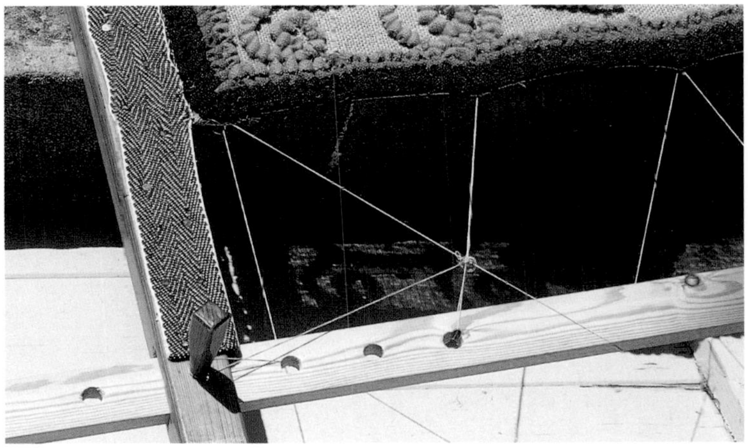

2 Sew a 3.5 cm (1½ in) hem all round the hessian with tacking thread. Sew long sides to webbing with button thread. Stretch hessian as tightly as possible across frame, secure with tin tacks, and tack long sides. If hessian is loose it is very difficult to work and tends to distort.

3 Starting with the border, hold the wool at the back with your left hand (if you are right-handed), and hook it through from the front at 3 mm (⅛ in) intervals, leaving a 1 cm (½ in) loop. Then work main motif.

4 Fill in background with lively variations of colour and directions of work. Use curves to depict a nice windy sky. Let your imagination have free rein at this stage.

5 Work on until you finish. Emma does not listen to the radio: 'I listen to that glorious sound of silence.' She can finish a 60×90 cm (2×3 ft) rug in a week.

6 Emma pulls through the final loops for a background of farm hay. To finish your rug snip stitches attaching the webbing, and then throw the finished rug on the floor.

*F*ELTWORK

Right *Shades of an English summer in a herbaceous border of felt to tie around your neck.*

Below *A pyramid of juvenile jesters' slippers, all unabashed primary colours and bold zigzag stitching.*

Far right *An explosion of pure colour to demonstrate the rainbow richness of felt – nothing matches it.*

Felt – 'A kind of cloth or stuff made of wool, or of wool and fur or hair, fulled or wrought into a compact substance by rolling and pressure, with lees or size' – was first mentioned by Ælfric at the turn of the first millenium. Felt was the first textile ever produced and has been around ever since man discovered that animal hair and sheep's wool could be induced, by soaking and shrinking, to produce a thick, matted waterproof fabric which does not fray. It was, according to one legend, St Clement who first made this discovery, by stuffing his boots with wool to keep his feet warm – the combination of wool, warmth, pressure and moisture created felt.

A felt carpet, embroidered with turtles and fish, afforded comfort in the afterlife to the Mongolian chieftains who died at least one hundred years before Christ. Magnificent felt appliquéd wall hangings and saddle linings depicting animal hunts, and a seated felt goddess holding a sacred branch, were found at a seventh- to second-century BC burial site in Siberian Pazyryk.

Genghis Khan was resplendent in a felt crown. The nomadic Russians who roamed the Steppes from the Balkans to the Gobi Desert made use of felt for both clothes and temporary homes; and Central Asian nomads live in huge felt tents or *yurts*. Eskimos still keep out the cold by wearing felt legwarmers, and traditional Scandinavian and Yugoslavian jackets and waistcoats are decorated with bright swirls of felt appliqué (often in red to repel witches), which represent the sun, spirals and the tree of life. You may still find Greek brides wearing the *podia*, the

Above *These leopardskin pillbox hats (and tiger and zebra) endanger no wild animals: a simple and dramatic shape in dyed felt by Heather Belcher.*

gold embroidered red felt apron, which endows its magic properties to childbirth, whilst in Czechoslovakia, thick felted wool coats are regulation winter wear.

In fourteenth-century Britain, the historian, Camden talks of Edward II prancing about in felt boots. By the fifteenth century people had started to sport felt hats; in the sixteenth they wore felt cloaks, capes and mantles; in the seventeenth they snored beneath felt blankets; in the eighteenth felt bags were *de rigueur*; and in the nineteenth, felt shoes were an aid both to warmth and stealth.

Charming and unpretentious pieces of felt jewellery had been made to add a touch of glamour to the wardrobes of ingenious and impecunious European women since the turn of the twentieth century, and in the 1920s, 30s and 40s, felt enjoyed a resurgence in popularity. It was rediscovered as an obliging and decorative material that did not fray and could be cut into any shape. Mats and cushions, work bags and handbags, tea cosies and coverlets in bold felt appliqué began to leaven the prevailing cream and *eau-de-Nil* of pre-war décor. For a while all kinds of objects, necessary or not, were made from appliquéd felt. A rash of felt bookmarks, calendars, napkin rings, needlebooks, teapot holders and cases for measuring tapes broke out everywhere. The felt fad finally culminated in that 1950s sartorial abomination, the circular felt skirt, guaranteed to bestow the illusion of hugely excessive hips on the most slender wearer.

Despite its fall from grace in recent times, felt still has a number of unique qualities: the bright clear colours combine well, and the naïve charms of appliquéd felt flowers lend a nostalgic innocence to whatever they touch.

Below right *Bucolic bliss – a pair of Gloucester Old Spots rootling peacefully in a textured felt hanging by Jean Rudland.*

CLARE *B*EATON'S *F*LOWERED *F*ELT *H*AT

Clare Beaton owes her bold graphic fluency to years of working as a designer for children's television, making masks, hangings and puppets. She later reverted to her initial training in illustration and graphic design to illustrate a number of books. She has always enjoyed making things – apart from the raffia mats to which she was condemned at school – but her interest in felt began by chance when she bought her young daughter a red dress, and had a notion that it might be greatly improved by the addition of a bright collar. This turned out so successfully that she tackled a pair of slippers, and then some gloves. Then Clare began to work on her book on felt work. 'I love doing it. Felt has been neglected and can be wonderful – the colours are so rich and dense. It's so easy to work with. You don't even have to be able to sew. It's terribly therapeutic.' She advocates experimentation by adding different bits and pieces as you fancy: feathers, buttons, beads, different coloured threads, ribbon, tassels and sequins. 'Once you have begun, you should do your own thing. Your hat doesn't have to look like mine.'

Above left *Clare at work on a pair of diminutive slippers, her workspace a dazzling rainbow of clear, bright felts, braids and trimmings. This is the sort of inspiring jumble that makes your fingers itch to snip and stitch.*

Above right *A feline chase on the original collar of the original red dress that started Clare in the felt business. Hat, gloves and slippers (all eminently copyable) came later.*

PROJECT:

Clare Beaton's Flowered Felt Hat

A hat as bright and simple as a nursery school drawing, with a touch of Renaissance-style decoration.
To make Clare's pillbox hat you will need:

Materials

- Black felt measuring at least 22.5×100 cm (9×40 in)
- Scraps of tan, scarlet, raspberry-pink and mulberry felt
- Garnet-red double knitting wool
- 4-ply wool in turquoise, emerald, daffodil-yellow, royal-blue
- Terylene wadding
- Black sewing cotton

Tools

- Scissors
- Darning and sewing needles
- Pins

Right *Leaf template to trace.*
Below *Cut out the felt to the following dimensions.*

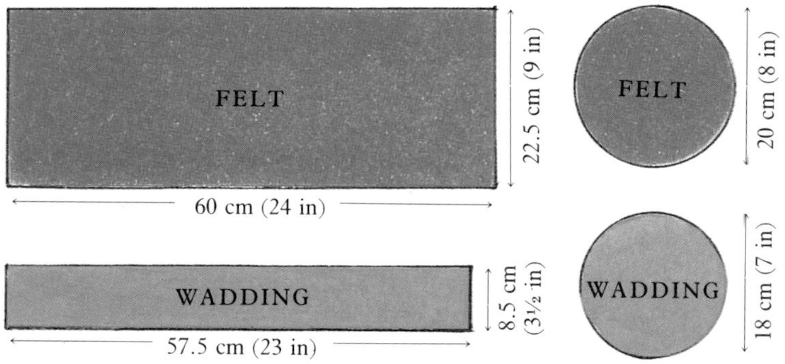

1 Measure your head where you expect the hat to sit most comfortably (Clare wears hers on the back of her head, where she measures 57.5 cm (23 in)). Cut a strip of black felt to your measurement plus 2.5 cm (1 in) for join and seam allowances, and 22.5 cm (9 in) wide. Doubled ove… this will form the sides. … rip of wadding … (23 in) long and … to inter…

2 Cut a circle for the crown to fit: in Clare's case 20 cm (8 in) in diameter, and another circle 2.5 cm (1 in) smaller. Cut a circle of wadding to the smaller size. With small stitches and black sewing cotton, fold and sew the sides … and sandwich the c… ers together as show… ving an unwadded seam allo… ance at the crown and down the back seam. Join the back seam with small and neat stitches.

3 Pin and ease the crown to fit the sides and oversew together invisibly with black thread. With garnet-red double knitting wool and a darning needle, make a line of even decorative oversewing around the join at the crown.

4 Using the template provided on the opposite page as a guide, carefully cut out 2 leaves from each of the different pieces of felt so that you have 8 leaves in all.

5 Using 4-ply wool, decorate the mulberry leaves with turquoise veins, the raspberry leaves with emerald dots, the tan leaves with royal-blue dashes and scarlet leaves with daffodil-yellow veins.

6 Pin the leaves on to the hat, spacing them evenly and alternately facing up and down and at an angle, ensuring that no 2 matching leaves are next to each other. Attach with 4-ply wool to the outer layer of felt only, using royal-blue overstitching for the raspberry, emerald for the tan, turquoise for the scarlet and yellow for the mulberry.

7 Add random 4-ply stars using your four different yarn colours for the finishing touch. Wear with panache.

*K*ITCHENCRAFT

The kitchen has always been the comforting heart of the home. The country kitchen was traditionally a magnet for drinking, eating, playing, the inevitable domestic chores and above all, good conversation. Few people nowadays crochet beaded milk-jug covers or need a meatsafe with panels of punched tin, but the irresistible urge remains to enhance the quotidian business of life with splashy spongeware jugs, baskets and bowls set against harmonizing painted wooden shelves.

Above *A satisfyingly bulbous basket woven in stripes of biscuit, orange and olive.*

Right *The quintessential kitchen dresser is home to an eclectic collection of brightly painted and sponged china.*

COUNTRY FRESH
PIE
SPOONS

BASKETS

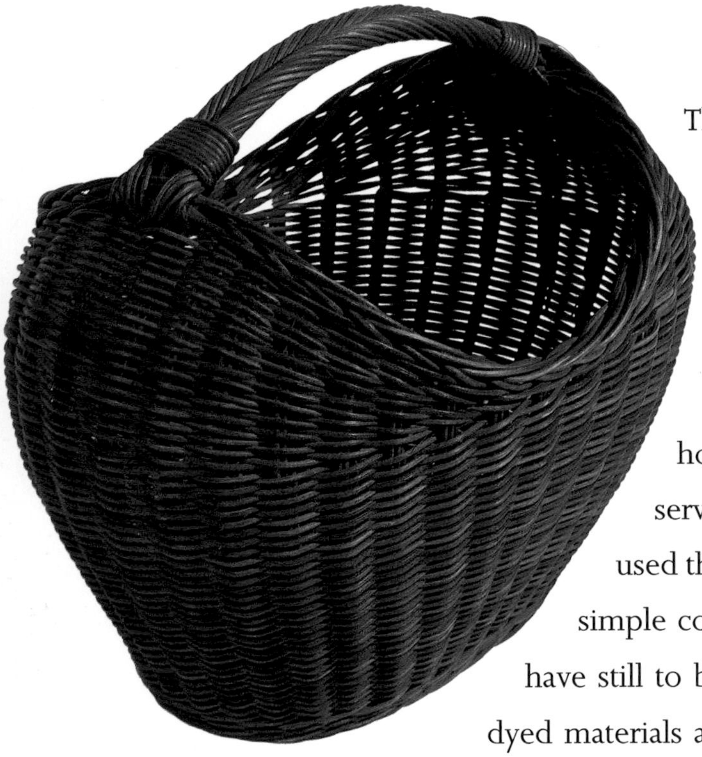

The North-American Indians are the basketmakers *par excellence*. They began some nine thousand years ago, and used whatever materials came to hand – coiled or split willow or hazel, cane, sheaves of grass and rush, the bark of trees and the roots of ferns, split and pounded ash, oak or hickory. They sealed them with resin to make water containers, or wove them tightly to make cooking pots into which a hot rock could be tossed to heat the contents. They made them flat to serve as plates and dishes, or openly woven to winnow grain. The Indians used three basic techniques – plaiting, twining and coiling, and within these simple confines they produced containers of a diversity and complexity that have still to be surpassed. They introduced sophisticated patterns by combining dyed materials and herringbone weaving, and the Algonquins painted their splints, or patterned them with potato cuts. The Indians of the North-west effected jazzy patterns by embroidering their work with dyed grass stems, or painting their curious conical hats with mysterious symbols. The Pomo Indians embellished their shallow coiled baskets with harlequin patterns of multi-

Above *Forest-green, cinnabar-red and a glaucous blue in a curvaceous and beautifully crafted dyed wicker basket by Lois Walpole.*

Right *Dyed willow urns to glorify your laundry. The smoothness of the cane gives a rich and satiny sheen.*

Far right *Sheaves of natural withies and some perfect examples of classic basketwork by Jenny Crisp and other craftspeople.*

coloured feathers and beads, adding the odd quail-feather tassel or shell pendant to add variety. If acorn mush is your thing, then the Pomo made the basket for it – tall and conical with a handsome zigzag of darker grasses. The genius survives, and some members of the Choctaw and the Mohawk tribes can still, if they have a mind to, execute a virtuoso turn with split cane or black ash.

The most fluent vernacular basketwork today probably comes from South-East Asia and developed from the ingenious use of the bamboo and rattan that grows there in lush abundance. A huge multiplicity of sizes and shapes of baskets are made, to answer just about every carrying or containing need – food, clothes, live animals and water are all transported or stored in baskets, made water-tight where necessary with beeswax or lacquer. Huge bamboo baskets serve as coracle-shaped boats. Whatever its intended purpose, the cane is soaked to make it malleable, and the finished basket is cured by smoke to harden it and make it pest-resistant. Thai basketmakers use the

Above *An unmistakable and traditional Gallic offshoot of the international fraternity of basket-makers. Here, the willow is peeled, prior to making capacious baskets bearing a close resemblance to American bushel and peck, white-oak split baskets.*

Right *Perfect simplicity, the hallmark of the Shakers, abounds in this array of baskets made of blonde pounded ash splints, a style and technique originally learned from the native American Indians.*

same three techniques as the Indians, and colour their work by burying it, in the case of rattan, which turns it black, or by dipping it in indigo or dragon's blood (the scarlet rattan-fruit resin). Woodsmoke dyes it dark brown and onion skins yellow.

In Europe and America, there are traditions for the rational, utilitarian-style oak swill-baskets, trugs, and sturdy containers of dark or peeled willow. New England baskets have elegant swing handles. Most Shaker baskets – cat-head, spoon and deaconess, for example – which are shaped over a mould, predictably combine the useful and the beautiful. Appalachian white-oak baskets have good strong handles and endearingly rotund shapes, presumably dictated by their functions. Market and pie baskets are self-explanatory and describe an appealingly down-home sort of life. Gizzard baskets, on the other hand, may be taking this specialization a little too far for most tastes.

Above *A huge split-ash basket, just right for quilt storage, in a room of Shaker plainness. The sage-green and russet paint and plank furniture contribute to the puritanical mood.*

Baskets are, at their best, a perfect marriage of form and function. These days they threaten to become works of art so rarified that their purpose has become negligible in the heady excitement of experimenting with new materials and shapes. The homely names have been jettisoned in favour of titles as enigmatic as Japanese haiku. Brilliant sculptural creations in copper wire, rubber, Plexiglas and acrylic, stun with their virtuoso dexterity, but have a pretentious edge that compares unfavourably with the insouciance of African Imbenge baskets made from brightly coated telephone wire – beautiful, and you can keep your lemons in them too. Baskets have always been art objects, and in making good use of a perfectly balanced, fastidiously finished Shaker apple basket, or a rough and husky Amana willow log basket, one can enjoy the grace of their makers without recourse to reverential awe and a gold Amex card.

*L*OIS *W*ALPOLE'S *F*RUIT *B*ASKET

The strikingly coloured fruit basket that forms our project has been specially devised by the internationally acclaimed basketmaker, Lois Walpole. Lois experiments with materials and colours to weave rainbow designs from humble cardboard, dyed cane, willow and plastic packaging tape, or in fond recollection of a feast, from corks and Camembert boxes, scallop and mussel shells linked together with wire. For the dubious beginner, her methods have the wonderful advantage of being very easy and cheap. If you embark on a cardboard bowl and it turns out a little wobbly round the edges, you can knock up another for the price of a dab of paint. Emboldened by success, you could try using different colours, or weaving a more elaborate shape. You might embark on something more ambitious, incorporating the odd shell or feather. You might fancy trying sharp stripes or random dots, or making a tiny bowl exploiting the patterns of fine printed card. The basic technique mastered, you can adapt the design to suit yourself and your intentions.

Sanctimonious is not a word that one would apply to Lois Walpole, but in her work she does use material from renewable sources wherever possible. 'Basketmaking is one of the few manufacturing industries that can honestly say it causes little or no harm to the environment.' Her baskets do much better than that – anyone who can so triumphantly combine the beautiful and the useful, who can bring joy to the more mundane aspects of life, such as dirty washing or table-laying, deserves every accolade.

PROJECT: *LOIS WALPOLE'S FRUIT BASKET*

Lois Walpole's fruit basket is a shallow woven vessel made from corrugated cardboard – simple, cheap and brilliantly coloured.

To make this rainbow-coloured basket you will need:

- 1 corrugated cardboard box, measuring at least 102 cm (40 in) around the girth and 41 cm (16 in) deep
- 4 or 5 different coloured acrylic paints
- old sponges or brushes
- one piece of plywood or stiff card measuring 46×4.5 cm (18×1¾ in), tapered equally for 15 cm (6 in) at both ends down to a width of 2 cm (¾ in) for a template
- metal rule and craft knife
- stapler and staples
- 1 plate, measuring 28 cm (11 in) diameter as a template
- 4 bulldog clips or clothes pegs
- scissors
- hole puncher
- leather needle and strong cotton or plastic cord, 3 m (3¼ yd) long
- acrylic varnish to seal

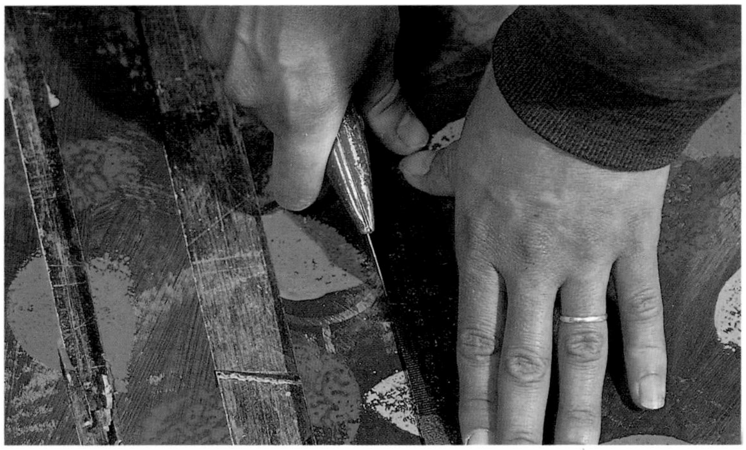

1 Open the box out and lay flat. Cut out a rectangle at least 102×41 cm (40×16 in). Apply colour, building up bright, transparent layers of acrylic paint. Leave to dry .

With a craft knife, cut your cardboard into 9 strips, 102 cm (40 in) long and 4.5 cm (1¾ in) wide. Cut across the corrugations not along them. Set aside 1 strip for the rim, and cut the rest in half 51 cm (20 in) long.

2 Draw around the template on all 16 strips and cut to shape. This is important because it makes the basket curve up. Rub the strips, paint-side up, over the edge of a table to soften them.

Start weaving by folding 2 strips in half crossways. Make a mark on the edge of each. Lay 1 down and the other across it at right angles with the marks visible and next to each other. This marks the centre.

3 Lay the 3rd strip over the 2nd (at right angles to it and parallel with the 1st.) The 4th strip goes in parallel with the 2nd, over the 3rd and under the 1st. As you weave, secure overlapping pieces with clips. Gradually you will see that the basket begins to curve up. Stop when you have woven 8 strips in each direction, making sure your marks stay central and that the strips all line up with each other around the edges.

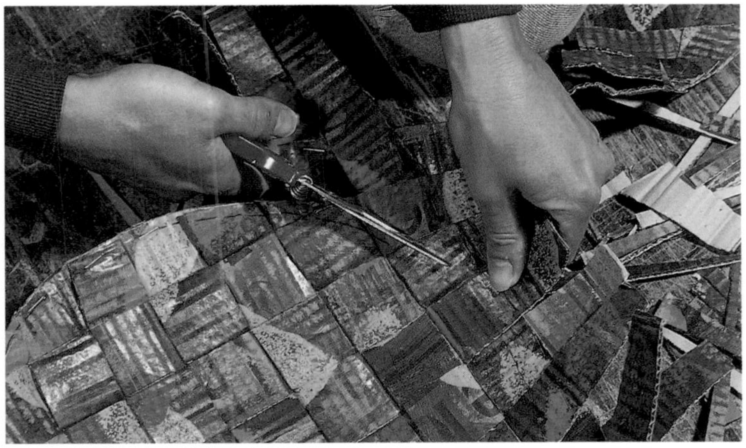

4 Position the template plate on the centre of the weave. The weave should overlap it slightly. Still holding the plate centrally on the weave, draw round it with a felt-tip pen to create the shape of your basket. Staple neatly all round the inside of this pen line to secure all the ends. With a sharp pair of scissors, carefully cut out the plate shape between 5 mm (1/4 in) and 1 cm (1/2 in) above the line of staples.

5 Take your reserved strip of cardboard and with the back of a pair of scissors, dent it down the centre of the back of the strip. Fold it in half all the way along. Use both hands to bend it into a circle shape.

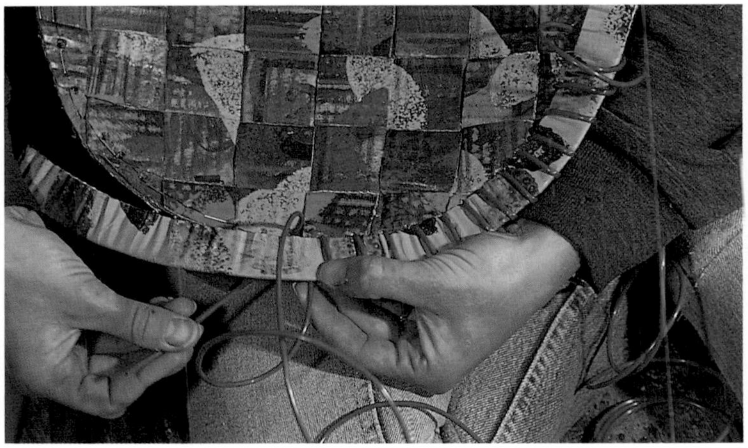

6 Punch a line of holes at 2 cm (3/4 in) intervals all round the rim just inside the staples with a hole-puncher or a compass point. Keep the holes in a fairly straight line. Thread your leather needle with strong plastic or cotton cord and sew the folded card rim neatly on to the basket. If you want to put more holes in the rim, you will need more cord but 3 m (3 1/4 yd) should be adequate for holes spaced at 2 cm (3/4 in).

7 When you have sewn the rim on all the way round, and are back at the beginning again trim the card rim so that it slots into the cavity of the other end. Finally, give the basket a coat of matt acrylic varnish.

*F*LOORCLOTHS

Floorcloths and oilcloths were much favoured in the United States from the mid-seventeenth century onwards. Defined in *Webster's Dictionary* as: 'A covering for floors made by treating a strong open canvas with successive coats of linseed-oil paint, smoothing with pumice after each application, and finally printing from blocks as in calico printing', they were the practical precursor to linoleum. In 1821, a more poetic recipe for oilcloth was described thus: 'Take drying or burnt linseed oil, set it on the fire, and dissolve in it some good rosin or gum-lac . . . you may either work it by itself, or add to it some colour, as verdigris for green, or umber for a hair colour, white-lead and lamp-black for grey or indigo and white for light blue.'

Below *A bright Caribbean floorcloth, all lemons and melon slices, in a cheerful fruit salad for the floor.*

Floorcloths were cheap to make. They could be stencilled or painted with geometric motifs, naturalistic or stylized flowers, and their designs could be as colourful and highly patterned as the ingenuity of their creator would allow. They lasted well, kept draughts at bay, and were easy to clean. What more could you ask from a rectangle of canvas?

Far right *A patchwork of many patterns, stencilled and aged and painted and gilded, with a touch of heraldry, a hint of Gauguin, a Pennsylvania Dutch tulip or two and the merest suggestion of a William Scott tablescape.*

Originally, wooden floors both in Great Britain and the United States were either sprinkled with sand and swept bare, or warmed with matting, woven or plaited from sedge, straw or rushes. When Turkish carpets first made their appearance in the homes of the very rich, they were thought too precious to be used on the floor, and tended to be draped sumptuously over tables or hung on walls. In the mid-seventeenth century floorcloths began to deck the boards; made of heavy sailcloth, they were stiffened with starch and then painted with black and white fake tiles, or even marblized to imitate

Right Sponged and spattered powder-blue oilcloth with crisp white stencilled swags and border for a children's bedroom. Other small touches, including a garter-stitch afghan and patchwork cushion, proclaim this as a crafts haven.

the floors of Renaissance palaces. Very occasionally, a more daring colour scheme was tried, such as red and yellow, but until the eighteenth century people were loath to depart from the established convention.

Floorcloths were exported from Great Britain to America in the eighteenth century, using patterns that are believed to have been copied from a century earlier. In one of the few surviving references, Alexander Wetherstone advertised himself as the proprietor of 'Ye Painted Floor Cloth and Brush in Portugal Street, near Lincoln's Inn back gate. 1763', and his sign shows a black and white diamond-patterned floorcloth, with a solid border and a compass in the centre. The compass motif may hark back to the fact that oilcloth had long been a sailor's best defence against a howling sou'wester gale. In the mid-eighteenth century, exported floorcloths included: 'Plain, Ornamented, Check, Matt and Carpet Patterns, Entirely New', and the paint was advertised as being treated against cracking or peeling.

There followed an outbreak of bright patterns including the traditional tulips of the Pennsylvania Dutch, and by the nineteenth century, stencils were commonly used for the complex repeats of circles within squares and delicate borders that embellished both floorcloths and painted floors. Stencils became a passion, and besides the familiar nineteenth-century striped and flowered wall designs, they were applied to homespun cotton for bed hangings, tablecloths, counterpanes and muslin curtains. Itinerant painters wandered the land, painting walls, floors, carpets and furniture to emulate costly wallpaper, inlay and carpets – a skill which declined in the mid-nineteenth century with the advent of the Industrial Revolution and mass-produced goods to answer every need.

Above *Sophisticated tapestry colours and stencilled laurel swags make a floorcloth that has nothing naïve about it – much of its success is due to the muted colours of the border and the broken texture of the cinnabar red.*

Very little documentation remains for floorcloths – researchers have to rely on the careful observation of family portraits and naïve paintings of interiors for visual clues as to the appearance and colours of traditional designs. Patchwork had an influence on patterns, and the classic geometric patchwork designs still lend themselves well to floorcloths.

Although floorcloths were superseded by linoleum and mass-produced carpet, they still make a more inspired contribution to bathroom or kitchen than any factory-made alternative. Aside from the traditional motifs of tulips, wreaths, 'tiles' and leaves, this blank canvas presents a wonderful opportunity to create a personal coat-of-arms, perhaps incorporating your family or pets. Alternatively you might wish to celebrate a birth, or the coming of spring, with a carpet of forget-me-nots; or you may simply decide to emulate a priceless Persian rug by the simpler and less labour-intensive means of paint and canvas.

Right *A corner of Christine's workroom, resplendent with floorcloths in rich warm colours and crisp geometrical patterns. Decorations and motifs include elegant and authentic diamonds, stars, compasses, and cheerfully ubiquitous Pennsylvania Dutch tulips.*
Far right *Christine in her working gear, surrounded by pots of well-used brushes and a stack of magazines for reference and inspiration.*
Below *Template for the two colourways for Christine's stars.*

*C*HRISTINE *S*MITH'S *D*IAMOND *F*LOORCLOTH

Christine Smith has a fascination with history. She has worked for many historical preservation groups, and time and again she came across references to floorcloths in historic inventories, but of the things themselves, not a trace remained. Not to be daunted, she confronted this little challenge with determined research into old paintings and eighteenth-century pattern books. Here she found a feast of diamonds with fake marbling and chequerboards – all very geometric and architectural. Mariners' compass points and pieced quilt designs were also recycled by Christine into designs for floorcloths. But a stint of painting at the Art Institute of Chicago encouraged an originality of approach: 'Painted blanket chest patterns work really well as runners too, with a geometric overlay.'

Wherever possible her work has a spontaneous hand-worked quality about it – one of the reasons that she does not use stencils is that they tend to look mechanical. Her own preference is for eighteenth-century designs and early folk art, but the trouble is that she does such an excellent pastiche of quaintly charming old-fashioned naïve art, that dogs and rabbits will just creep in.

PROJECT: *Christine Smith's Diamond Floorcloth*

Colours rich and regal, in a floorcloth that puts history at your feet.

To make Christine Smith's dramatic diamond floorcloth you will need:

Materials

- No. 8 heavy cotton duck or canvas (sold through canvas manufacturers or theatrical supply companies) to your chosen size – allowing for shrinkage
- Off-white latex primer
- Latex paints: dark red, navy, off-white and gold metallic
- Masking tape
- Clear satin-finish water-based varnish

Tools

- Pencil
- Graph paper
- Paint rollers and pans: 1 for paint; 1 for clear varnish
- Assortment of brushes – bristle and sponge
- Glue gun
- Scissors
- Right-angle and straight edge
- Template of star pattern

1 Prime canvas on flat surface using roller. Draw on design and trim to size allowing 2.5 cm (1 in) hem on all sides. Fold this over, mitre corners and seal with glue gun. Paint entire floorcloth with 2 base coats of off-white latex. Mask edges of diamond pattern with tape and apply navy paint in one direction only using dry bristle brush. Keep edges clean and crisp looking.

2 Use sponge brush to paint dark red border. Allow to dry. Use sponge brush to paint navy borders. Be sure to cover edge of floorcloth with paint – at least 2 coats will be necessary to cover the borders.

3 Decorate the centre of each off-white diamond with dark red stars, using a star-shaped template for the outline.

4 Detail stars with navy and gold metallic paint using fine brush. Allow to dry. Apply 3 coats of water-based varnish using a clean roller.

CHIMNEY BOARDS

Below *A proud trompe l'œil cat, surrounded by a vibrant display of summer flowers, occupies a position of honour in front of the fireplace.*

Far right *Animals have always been a popular subject for chimney boards. Here, a placid, life-sized sheep adds a bucolic touch to an old stone fireplace.*

From the eighteenth century onwards, painted wooden figures found their way into many homes, gardens, shops and alehouses in Great Britain and the United States. Wooden maids sat quietly by the fire peeling apples, and soldiers in minutely observed military garb guarded front hallways. Greyhounds pranced in unused fireplaces, and North American Indians with feather head-dresses lured passing smokers into tobacco shops. Gardeners leaned on their spades among flowered platts, and the lady of the house in her Sunday best plied an unenthusiastic broom as an example of virtuous toil for the benefit of her servants. The human figures and animals were often life-sized or larger, constructed very simply of tongued and grooved pine boards held together with battens, and mounted on a right-angled base. The cut-out figures, referred to as dummy boards, were then sanded or covered in paper or canvas, and the whole thing painted with every detail of face, hair and clothing carefully recorded.

These figures had various functions, chief of which was amusement: Thomas Gainsborough painted a bucolic figure, Thomas Peartree, to lounge on his garden wall and give a fright to passers-by. Gilbert White, being an impecunious parson with ideas above his means had a twelve-foot-high *trompe l'œil* statue of Hercules painted to impress visitors to his garden in Hampshire. Dummy boards had more utilitarian roles too – they were used to direct the way to drinking parlours and restaurants, as they still are today, and they were sometimes fitted with holders for lanterns and candles to illuminate dark corners.

WINE
COOLER

They were also hung outside shops to indicate the wares within, of which today's pub signs are the most illustrious relic. Hogarth (in his inimitable and witty way) dabbled with signboards, showing them finally in an exhibition in 1762. He described the art thus: 'Humour is confessedly one of the chief characteristics of the English nation . . . To an Artist of our own Country, and our own Times, we owe the Practice of enriching Pictures with Humour, Character, Pleasantry and Satire.' Four years later, hanging signs were prohibited because of the casualties caused when they dropped on the heads of innocent pedestrians in the street below. Much later, in the 1930s people liked to animate their gardens with lawn ornaments – alarming wooden dogs, brilliant peacocks and geese. These days life-sized, two-dimensional Holstein cows can be seen, peacefully cropping the grass in front of an upstate New York farm.

Another separate use was as chimney or fire boards, blocking the fireplace in summer to give a more appealing aspect than a cold and empty grate. At first, irregularly shaped dummy boards were placed in front of the fireplace, simply by way of decoration. Some were painted predictably, and somewhat pointlessly, with logs and a blazing fire, or to mimic bouquets of roses, tulips and passion flowers complete with butterflies – a reminiscence of the eighteenth-century custom of filling the empty grate with a vase of cut flowers. Many sported *trompe l'œil* animals – a favourite dog, primly self-satisfied cat or troughing piglet with a roguish eye. They were painted to match the room, or with seascapes, pastoral countryside views or baskets of fruit. Eventually people realized that if the boards were cut precisely to fit the surround, they would not only cheer the summer months, but also stop draughts and falling soot, birds' nests, racoons, bats, insects and anything else that was liable to fall down the chimney. Stencils, découpage, fabric and wallpaper were all used to enliven the boards, surrounded by frames of carved wood or *faux* blue and white Delft tiles. Come the winter, these works of art would be wiped down and relegated to the attic for another season.

Above *Painted wooden figures such as this lady, resplendent in her finest crinoline, have been used for centuries to add colour and a touch of humour.*
Far left *A vibrant display of colourful spring daffodils enlivens a grate.*

*E*mma *W*hitfield's *F*eline *C*himney *B*oard

Emma Whitfield comes from a family of painters, and her earliest memories are of a nomadic two-year sojourn living in a camper-van in Spain, Morocco and France. This was followed by ten years of living in a narrow-boat, *Alice*, in Aylesbury until she left to study fine art at art school. The strong, rich, graphic exuberance of traditional narrow-boat painted decoration has had a major influence on her style. She favours strong colours, and enjoys the rotund naïvety of the classic nosegays which decorated the boats that plied the canals of Great Britain. There is something of the narrow-boat baroque ethos too, in her recommendation to use screens, walls, trays, boxes, doors and door-frames, furniture, cupboards, lampshades and jewellery blanks as surfaces to deck with découpage, which she uses as an expedient alternative to freehand figurative paintings of fruit and flowers. Her favourite painters are Rembrandt, Vermeer, and Michelangelo, but she also draws inspiration from Dutch flower paintings, and the drawings of Watteau and Rodin. Her approach is a nicely pragmatic blend of a traditional look achieved by using contemporary technology. She is a great exponent of the photocopier, and waxes enthusiastic about the creative possibilities of hand-tinting huge black-and-white xeroxes.

Left *A friendly menagerie, complete with flowers and a chunky cupid or two, presents a seductive glimpse of the repertoire of colour and black-and-white xeroxes, wrapping paper, assorted paints, antiquing varnish and numerous whims and tricks that can embellish humble découpage.*

Far left *Emma surrounded by rolls of wrapping paper, which being just too good to use for banal present wrapping, are perfectly exploited and preserved by découpage.*

PROJECT: *EMMA WHITFIELD'S FELINE CHIMNEY BOARD*

A pair of undemanding pets requiring minimum care, to bestow an air of naïve charm to hearthside or window-sill. To make Emma's chimney board you will need:

Materials

- Colour photocopy of chosen image
- Thick mounting card. (For a larger chimney board, 9 mm (3/8 in) plywood would be suitable, primed back and front with a water-based acrylic primer)
- Wood glue, thinned with a few drops of water
- White spirit to clean brush
- Burnt umber acrylic paint
- Walnut-tinted varnish

Tools

- Stanley knife or scalpel
- Rectangle of stiff card or plastic to spread glue
- Scissors
- Paintbrush
- Access to colour photocopier

1 Enlarge your original (in this case a picture from a calendar) to the required size on a colour photocopier. Very large images can be copied in two halves and joined on the finished board. Cut out the image carefully with scissors.

2 Draw round cut shape on to card or plywood, leaving flaps at both sides so that the finished chimney board can stand upright. Cut out the shape very carefully with scalpel or Stanley knife, scoring the surface of the card first.

3 Spread diluted wood glue evenly on to the back of photocopied image with a rectangle of card. Attach immediately to the board starting with the horizontal base, and smoothing out any air bubbles with your hands from the centre outwards. Allow to dry.

4 Score side pieces to make hinges and fold back. Paint the back and edges of the card with burnt umber acrylic. If necessary, put the whole thing under a pile of books to flatten it. Finish off with a coat of walnut-tinted varnish.

*P*UNCHED *T*IN

Above The classic Paul Revere lantern, patterned with hearts and stars, through which candle-light twinkles, well protected from draughts. Right The painted, battered pie-safe beloved of every self-respecting American patriot and antique dealer. Far right Simple variants on candle-sconces, artfully rusted.

Metalwork in the United States was a somewhat crude affair until the eighteenth century, when Paul Revere discovered a method of rolling sheet metal. This meant that it no longer needed to be cast – which was cumbersome and costly – but could henceforth be raised, spun or stamped. At the same time, iron ore was discovered in Pennsylvania, and suddenly all sorts of possibilities presented themselves. If an object stands there long enough, someone in America will make a decorative feature out of it, and homely domestic metalwork did not escape the clutches of the improvers. The most banal everyday objects were transformed, from curlicued weathervanes to door hinges in the form of butterflies' wings and tulips; many-candled chandeliers hung from ceilings and even bootscrapers shaped like crouching cats clung to doorways.

Typically, the Pennsylvania Dutch achieved much with little, and made a glorious miscellany of objects out of tin (in fact they used thin sheet iron dipped briefly in tin to protect it from rust and to facilitate welding). With

this unpropitious material they made every kind of food container, trinket box, tray, sconce and candle holder, finished with transparent japanning, or by painting in red or black decorated with flowers, fruit and birds, or by punching. Toleware is the most ornate kind of tin, with its humble material disguised by skilful painting to look like inlay, marquetry or japanned lacquer. Decorative stencilling came into its own with toleware, and the usual glossy black background made a wonderful foil to misty gold bouquets and rich flower colours.

Left *This Christmas whimsy in gilded tin, is fun and quick to make with tin-snips, hammer and nail.*

Above *A more orthodox star panel in a sunny-yellow, distressed cabinet.*

The less glorious articles of patterned tin were usually unpainted, and wrought by a whitesmith (as opposed to a blacksmith who worked with iron and a forge). The punch did not always penetrate the tinware except when its purpose was to shed light or warmth – containers and trays just had indentations in relief. But footwarmers and Paul Revere lanterns were perforated with patterns as decorative as a frozen firework display, incorporating the whole gamut of stars, hex symbols, Catherine wheels, wagon wheels, patriotic eagles, marigolds and diamonds, all twinkling with light and heat. The lanterns with their conical tops gave the candle a firm and safe base, offering the flame some protection from wind, and the more holes they had punched, the more light they shed. Footwarmers were simple rectangular lidded boxes designed to hold hot coals, bricks or stones, which warmed frozen feet.

Punched tin is cheap and decorative, and it was not long before people started panelling their food storage cupboards and pie-safes with punched-tin hearts and sunrises, snowflakes and pineapples, which in the days before refrigeration not only kept food aerated and cool, but also kept insects and thieving animals at bay.

*J*AMES *P*ALOTAS' *P*IE-SAFE *P*ANEL

Left In his orderly Pennsylvanian workshop, James Palotas works surrounded by his range of traditional and original designs, along with samples of different metals and finishes. He is willing to tackle any size, and thinks nothing of cladding entire kitchens in twinkling tin. Right Shades of tin: Paul Revere, Shaker, Pennsylvania Dutch, Swiss, and even Mexican influences are incorporated here in simple lanterns and cones of light.

James Palotas first began making punched-tin lanterns as a hobby back in 1958, and together with his wife Marie has been collecting designs ever since. The couple share an ambition to elevate pierced metal from banal utility and exploit its decorative potential. James has traced this unjustly neglected craft back to its European origins, and discovered an antique example of a pierced-tin lantern decorated with pine boughs, shedding its sparkling light in a fifteenth-century tavern in the Vienna Woods. However, at home in his stream-bordered Victorian farmhouse in Williamsport, Pennsylvania, he is more likely to be found working on the numerous symmetrical geometric designs such as the snowflakes, hearts and tulips that are so beloved of the Americans.

'Punched tin is seeing a revival now. It is a beautiful, creative and surprisingly easy and inexpensive craft to learn.' Thanks to James Palotas, not only are antique pie-safes being rescued from the ignominy of tattered tin panels, but humble off-the-peg fitted kitchens can acquire resplendant character, the most banal of functional strip-lights can twinkle like the milky way, and the morning sun can cast a *diamanté* sparkle through pierced shutter panels.

Planning is vital to success, often taking longer than the work itself. The word 'tin' is misleading – pure tin is very soft and prohibitively expensive. Galvanized sheet metal is to be avoided, as it has an unsympathetic mosaic surface. The traditional material was 25×35 cm (10×14 in) panels of 'coke tin', a product of primitive plating methods that is virtually unobtainable today, which matured to an uneven dark grey and withstood rusting. Tin-plated sheet steel is an amenable substitute, and the brightness can be aged by removing some of the plating. Antique pie-safes often had the rough side out – if you use a punch, the perforations will not be too sharp, and it is safe to be authentic.

PROJECT: *J*AMES *P*ALOTAS' *P*IE-SAFE *P*ANEL

A delicate sprinkling of holes defines a traditional Pennsylvania Dutch pie-safe panel pattern to provide an original, charming and practical alternative to the more familiar kitchen clichés.

To make James Palotas' Pennsylvania Dutch pie-safe panel you will need:

Materials

- 28 gauge tin-plated sheet steel (copper, or brass can also be used)
- Strong paper for design
- Masking tape
- 60×60×2 cm (2 ft×2 ft×¾ in) smooth plywood or particle board
- Tacks
- Paint thinner
- Polyurethane varnish, satin, matt or gloss

Tools

- Ruler and pencil
- Compass
- Chinagraph pencil or pencil and carbon paper
- Nail punch for small round holes, chisels for slits
- 8 or 12 oz ballhammer
- Cotton gloves
- Rawhide mallet
- Soft cloth
- Sandpaper

1 Measure panel and design motif on paper, starting by drawing a guideline 2.5 cm (1 in) inside the edges. For safety, wrap the edges of the tin with masking tape, but be careful not to touch any part of the metal that will be visible – fingers leave marks on many metals. Work through the paper pattern wrapped tautly round the tin, or transfer the design with a Chinagraph pencil, or pencil and carbon paper.

2 Place the tin on a piece of plywood or particle board, working on a firm surface. You can secure the four corners of the tin and the pattern with tacks at this stage. Tap out the design with a nail punch and ballhammer, tapping lightly for small holes, and harder for larger holes. Use a chisel for variety.

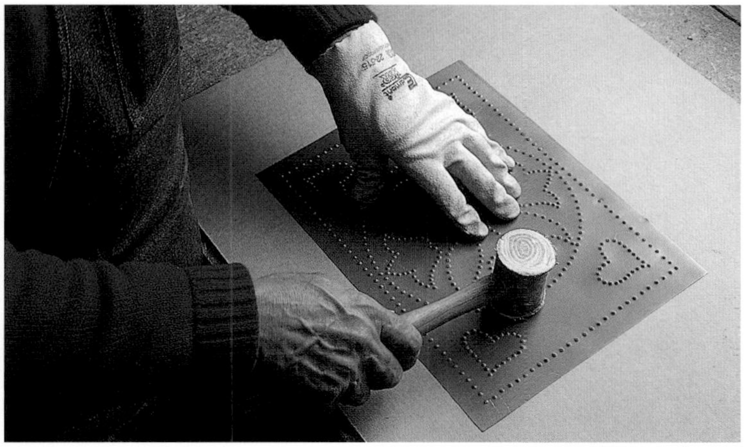

3 Wearing a glove to protect the surface of the tin from fingermarks, turn the panel and gently hammer out dents with rawhide mallet, which will not mark the tin further.

4 Wipe off guidelines if used with a soft cloth damped with paint thinner, and sand lightly. Seal with varnish.

*W*OODCRAFT

The fine arts of cabinet-making, marquetry, carving and turning require serious tools and expertise, but the humbler artefacts – the naïve animals, ingenious weathervanes, custom-built and brightly coloured containers, shelves and whatnots – are well within the range of the interested amateur. At this level, woodwork is speedy and produces a fine sense of achievement for very little angst. In fact, a session of peaceful whittling or painting is one of the most therapeutic antidotes to the stresses of life.

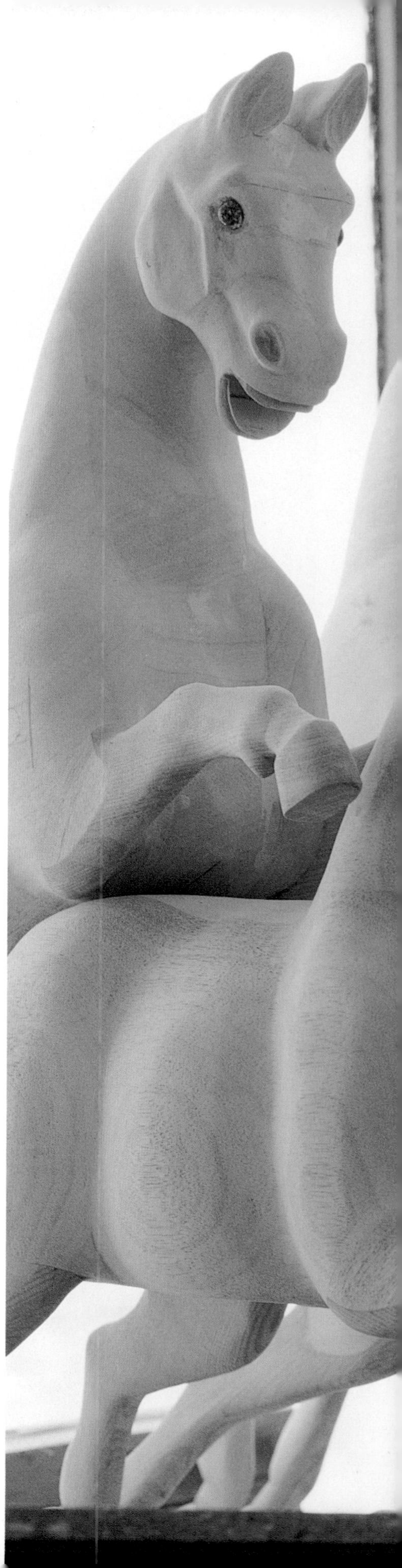

Above *Less is more. A classic example of the elegance of Shaker artefacts.*
Right *A production line of prancing horses, each one individually carved, awaiting paint and a pair of rockers.*

SHAKER AND AMISH WOODWORK

The philosophy of the Shakers – legendary for their espousal of simplicity, and the pure practical elegance of everything they made or used – has a relevance today that is both salutary and comforting. They did not make impractical things, but if an object were both necessary and useful, they did not hesitate to make it beautiful. Decoration was confined to what was both inherent in the design, and could be achieved without interfering with its function. You would have a long and fruitless search to find a solitary ugly Shaker object. Mother Ann Lee, who founded the communities, exhorted her followers to 'Put your hands to work, and your hearts to God and a blessing will attend you'. Everything the Shakers did was an act of homage, and it was Father Joseph Meacham of the New Lebanon community, who died in 1796, who coined the phrase: 'From each according to his ability, to each according to his need.'

Above *The perfect marriage of function and form: who but the Shakers could make a bucket beautiful; and who else would bother?*

Right *Detail of an oval box: a mute reminder that with hands applied to work and hearts devoted to God, perfection is achievable.*

Far right *A stack of Shaker boxes which delicately exploit the grain of differing woods and the worn patina of milk paint.*

Shaker community houses reflect the consummate marriage of beauty and function. Their spartan plainness makes the bright but subtle colours of furnishings, and the grace of the utensils within, all the more emphatic. A sense of order informs every aspect of Shaker life, and is embodied in their copious built-

Right *A few of the very basic essentials of Shaker life – there is nothing startling or stunning here, although the vibrant use of colour is surprising among such sober people. But the integrity and quiet beauty of every single Shaker object is a powerful antidote to the general philistine excess which surrounds twentieth-century mankind. The Shakers simply never touched anything ugly: everything from cutlery to coat-racks was designed to be perfect for its job, without superfluous detail, and made with extraordinary grace. However ill-supported their religious ideals, they have left a tangible legacy of excellence that in some measure counters one's despair at post-industrial man's passion for ugliness.*

in cupboards and drawers. As Mother Ann advised: 'Provide places for all your things, so that you may know where to find them at any time, day or night.'

Another rule of thumb was that all work should be undertaken in a spirit of perfectionism. Mother Ann told believers to work as if they had a thousand years to live, and as they would if they knew they were to die tomorrow. Everything was made with care, the best materials for the job were used, and the best methods evolved over years of apprenticeship. The oval boxes with their perfectly fitting lids and graceful swallowtails, are made from a combination of pliable maple shaped on a mould for the sides, and amenable, easily available pine for the top and bottom. The bevelled swallowtails, cut with a knife using a metal template, absorb the expansion and contraction brought about by heat and damp. Copper tacks are used to pin the box together, so as not to stain the wood. Every part is smoothed and gently rounded, and minute attention to detail means that a genuine Shaker box is a beautiful object to feel and use. 'Trifles make perfection, but perfection is no trifle' expressed the Shaker ethos.

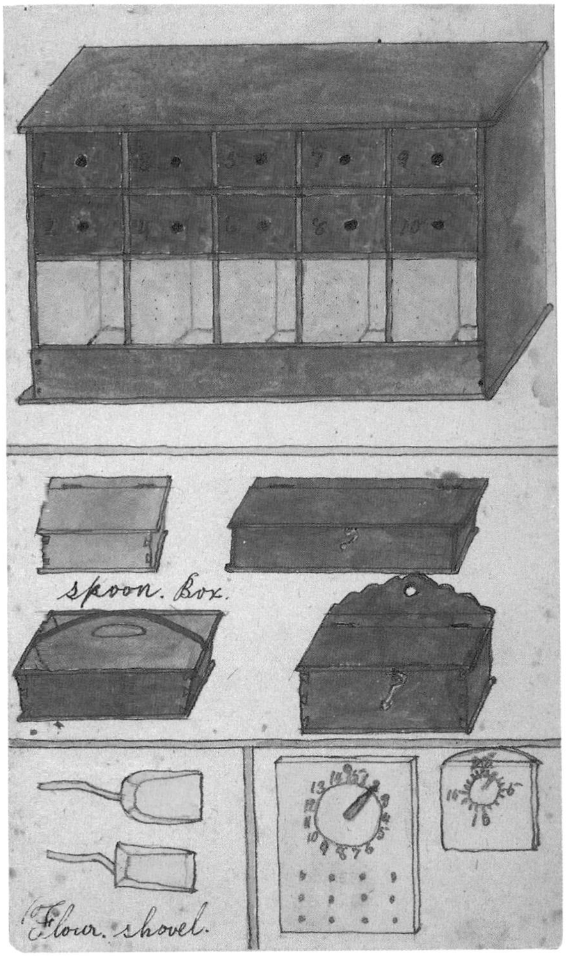

Above *A page from Henry Lapp's sketchbook, an Amish carpenter, deaf, dumb, and legendary for his handsome furniture designs and skilled craftsmanship. A few of his pieces still survive their maker – he died in 1913 – but somehow his furniture seems to date from a much earlier era.*

Of the many revered Shaker and Amish woodworkers, Henry Lapp has left the most endearing legacy. He was a deaf mute, and kept a record of his designs in a notebook, using pen-and-ink overlaid with washes of clear, bright colour. Lapp tackled all sorts of furniture and containers, from cutlery boxes to rabbit hutches, and besides their characteristic elegance, they have an air of deceptive approachability. 'Quick and easy' Shaker is a contradiction in terms, but there is no villainy in emulating the beauty and utility of their creations, and running up a handy trug in the spirit of the Shaker tradition. To quote a believer, 'A man can show his religion as much in measuring onions [or making trugs] as he can in singing glory halluah.'

MOIRA HANKINSON'S SOMERSET TRUG

Left Moira Hankinson conferring instant antiquity on a corn-yellow Somerset trug, surrounded by a reference collection of shape variants. Once mastered, the basic design can be adapted for a thousand uses. *Right* Brimming with spring produce, these simple trugs, painted in soft colours are the sort of objects that quickly become indispensable. They make flattering containers for just about anything, from love-letters to prize parsnips.

Moira Hankinson trained at the London College of Fashion, where she developed a penchant for stylish simplicity. After a long stint travelling in Europe and Africa, and living in America for a year, she returned to London where she taught and organized courses in Chelsea. But the call of the country proved very strong, and she and her husband, Nick, moved to Somerset, where their daughter Eleanor was later born. Whilst renovating their old cottage, they spent many happy hours combing the local antique shops and attending farm sales. Attracted by the simplicity of the country bits and pieces that they found, Moira designed a wooden container that could be painted using the colours that she had already used in her farmhouse kitchen. The trugs worked out so well that friends were keen to buy them. Moira and Nick work together – not always seeing eye to eye – but engaged in fruitful sparring, as the quality and charm of their work attests.

It is not a bad life for a pair of refugees from London, looking out at the wide blue skies over the Somerset Levels, watching the birds and the mists that suddenly steal across the flatlands: 'It has a magic that is good to wake up to in the morning. Living in a farmhouse inspired us; the original and largest Somerset trug would not have been born in a smaller house. When the weather's good, we get on our bicycles and go across the Levels.' Presumably with picnic-packed trugs strapped on the back.

Moira's trugs have a simple adaptability that suits any use you care to make of them: whether out in the garden, filled with fruit or vegetables in the kitchen, overflowing with magazines in the sitting room, fragrantly packed with soap and sponges in the bathroom, or bringing order to a chaos of make-up in a bedroom. They look good hung from beams, as a foil for flowers, or decked with tartan ribbons and a cargo of mince pies for a Christmas celebration.

PROJECT: *MOIRA HANKINSON'S SOMERSET TRUG*

A stylish interpretation of Shaker simplicity: easy to make, and perfectly embodying the ethos of beauty through utility. To make this elegant piece of history you will need:

Materials

- 150 cm (60 in) length of 100×7.5 mm (4×$\frac{5}{16}$ in) softwood timber sawn into 2×45 cm (18 in) lengths, and 2×28.5 cm ($11\frac{1}{2}$ in) lengths
- 125 cm (50 in) length of 75×7.5 mm (3×$\frac{5}{16}$ in) softwood timber sawn into 3×40.5 cm ($16\frac{1}{4}$) lengths
- 45 cm (18 in) length of 28×7.5 mm ($1\frac{1}{8}$×$\frac{5}{16}$ in) of softwood timber sawn into 2×22.5 cm (9 in) lengths

(Select timber for character of grain and knotting. Sizes refer to finished planed measurements.)

- 40 cm (16 in) of 2.25 cm ($\frac{15}{16}$ in) hardwood broom handle or dowelling
- 15 cm (6 in) of 6 mm ($\frac{1}{4}$ in) dowelling
- 1 cm ($\frac{1}{2}$ in) and 2 cm ($\frac{3}{4}$ in) copper or fine steel nails
- Waterproof wood glue
- Dark oak water-soluble fence paint
- Matt emulsion paint or distemper for the more adventurous. Modern water-based paints are designed to be hardwearing and easy to apply. Old paints, washes and distempers have a lower plasticity but higher pigment content, and are particularly suitable for distressing to simulate the effects of time and wear
- Rottenstone, dust or ochre acrylic paint can be used for distressing.
- Pine wax, dark or light

Tools

- Light hammer
- Nail punch
- Coarse and medium sandpaper and sanding block
- Ruler and pencil
- Saw
- Hand plane
- 2.5 cm (1 in) paintbrush
- Medium grade wire wool
- Polishing brush and cloth
- Drill, and sharp 6 mm ($\frac{1}{4}$ in) drill bit

Power tools, such as drill, sander and planer simplify the project, but are not essential.

1 Take 2×45 cm (18 in) lengths and 2×28.5 cm ($11\frac{1}{2}$ in) lengths cut from the 10 cm (4 in) wide timber. Mark the centre of each along one edge, and measuring outwards, mark 19.5 cm ($7\frac{7}{8}$ in) each side of the centre of the longer piece and 11 cm ($4\frac{3}{8}$ in) from the centre of the shorter. With pencil and ruler draw a line from these points to the outside corners to give the correct angle for the splay of the trug. Saw along the pencil lines, and you will end up with 2 side pieces measuring 45 cm (18 in) at the top and 39.5 cm ($15\frac{3}{4}$ in) at the bottom, and 2 end pieces measuring 28.5 cm ($11\frac{1}{2}$ in) along the top and 23 cm ($9\frac{1}{4}$ in) along the bottom. Plane top and bottom edges of all pieces so that when assembled the trug will have flat base and top.

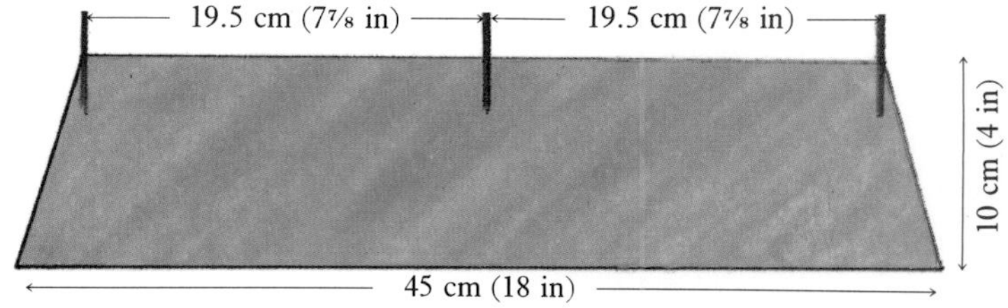

2 Lightly nail 2×2 cm (3/4 in) nails into each end of the short pieces, 2 cm (3/4 in) from top and bottom and 9 mm (3/8 in) from the sawn edge. Apply wood glue liberally to the sawn ends of the longer pieces. Assemble the sides as shown in the photograph above, and tap the nails home. Use a nail punch to drive the nails just below the surface.

3 Take 3 lengths of 7.5 cm (3 in) timber 40.5 cm (16¼ in) long for the bottom of the trug. Ensuring that the base is square, apply wood glue to the base of the trug and nail the 3 lengths in place to form the base. Drive the nails just below the surface. Leave to dry for the manufacturer's recommended drying time.

4 When all the sides are absolutely dry, place the trug on a level surface and plane any excess material from the base edges, for a smooth and slightly rounded finish. When planing across the grain, work away from the corners to prevent splitting.

5 Cut 2×22.5 cm (9 in) lengths of 2.8 cm (1⅛ in) timber for the handle supports. Using a plane, round off the tops to fit the handle, and finish with sandpaper to fake wear. Apply glue to the bottom 7.5 cm (3 in) of handle supports, and using 1 cm (½ in) nails, fix to centre of sides of trug, ensuring that they are positioned at an angle of 90 degrees to the sides.

6 Hold the broomhandle against the top of the handle uprights and with a pencil carefully mark the angle of splay to allow handle to fit snugly within uprights and approximately 6 mm (¼ in) from top. Cut to size, and nail to uprights using 2×2 cm (¾ in) nails for each end, avoiding the centre of the handle.

7 Holding assembled trug on its side, drill 2×6 mm (¼ in) holes through handle upright and body of trug. Drill a further hole through top of upright and 2 cm (¾ in) into end of handle, avoiding the nails. Repeat on the other side. Cut 6 mm (¼ in) dowel to 2×3.5 cm (1½ in) lengths for handle, and 4×2 cm (¾ in) lengths for fixing handle to base. Apply glue to drilled holes and gently insert dowels using a hammer.

8 When completely dry, trim protruding dowel ends using a plane and sandpaper. Sand off all rough edges and smooth the corners to emulate years of wear.

9 Paint the underside of the trug with diluted dark oak water-soluble fence paint, using 1 part stain to 3 parts water.

10 When dry, paint remainder of trug with matt emulsion or distemper. Do not attempt to paint too evenly – brush marks and drips are part of the character of the final paint finish.

11 When dry, distress with sandpaper. Paint as shown with diluted fence paint or acrylic paint. Leave for about 10 minutes until almost dry. Rottenstone or any other ageing materials can be added directly to wet paint.

12 Wax the whole trug except for the underside, starting with the inside and working round to the outside before finishing with the handle. Apply the wax vigorously using wire wool to raise the surface of the paint and thereby mixing it with the wax. Pay special attention to the corners to give a patina of ancient grime.

13 After waxing, polish the whole trug inside and out using a brush, and finally buff with a soft cloth.

*W*OODEN *T*OYS

Right *A gaggle of extrovert poultry: smiling pull-along duck, a rooster of mysterious purpose and a hobby-duck for a diminutive passenger.*

Below *A carved cat frozen in mid-leap, forever pouncing on an exceptionally luckless beetle.*

Far right *The setting for a miniature period soap opera. A dolls' house presented by Queen Anne to the children at Heydon Hall to play with. The gilded and pinked leather shelf edgings are eminently copyable.*

One of the best things about being human is playing. Everyone needs to play, from the grandfather whittling Noah's ark animals in the front porch, to the baby hurling rattles out of his cot for an obliging sibling to fetch. Wood has been the best-loved material for toys since a fine wooden tiger with snapping jaws was carved in Egypt a couple of thousand years ago. Some time later, the young Aeschylus or Ovid could have whiled away the endless sunny afternoons in vine-shaded courtyards by roaring around on a hobby horse, or sailing flotillas of model boats across transparent blue Mediterranean waters.

Throughout fifteenth- and sixteenth-century Europe, the tribulations of an all-too-short childhood were tempered with an array of dolls, wooden cradles and painted soldiers. The seventeenth century witnessed the arrival of dolls' houses, or *les petits ménages*, as they were first known. These elaborate room sets were filled with tiny furnishings and far too precious to be entrusted to mere children.

By the eighteenth century, toys had become a serious feature of the market-place, particularly in Germany where itinerant entrepreneurs would travel from village to village, employing rural families

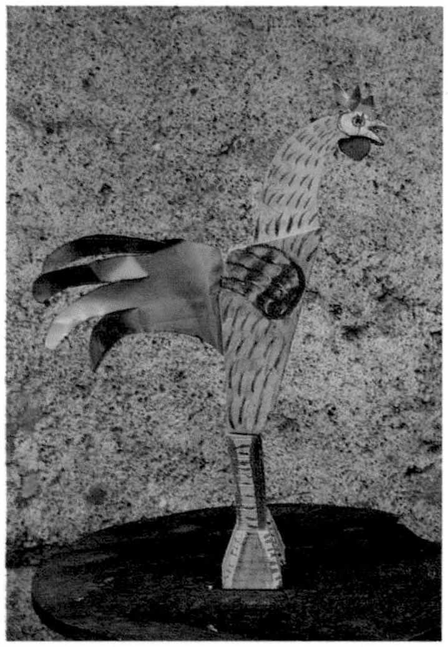

Above *A roughly painted hybrid wood and tin cockerel, crowing his wattles off.*

Right *Naïve and proud of it, an ornithologist's nightmare of an unidentifiable chunky duck, set off by a splendid painted shelf.*

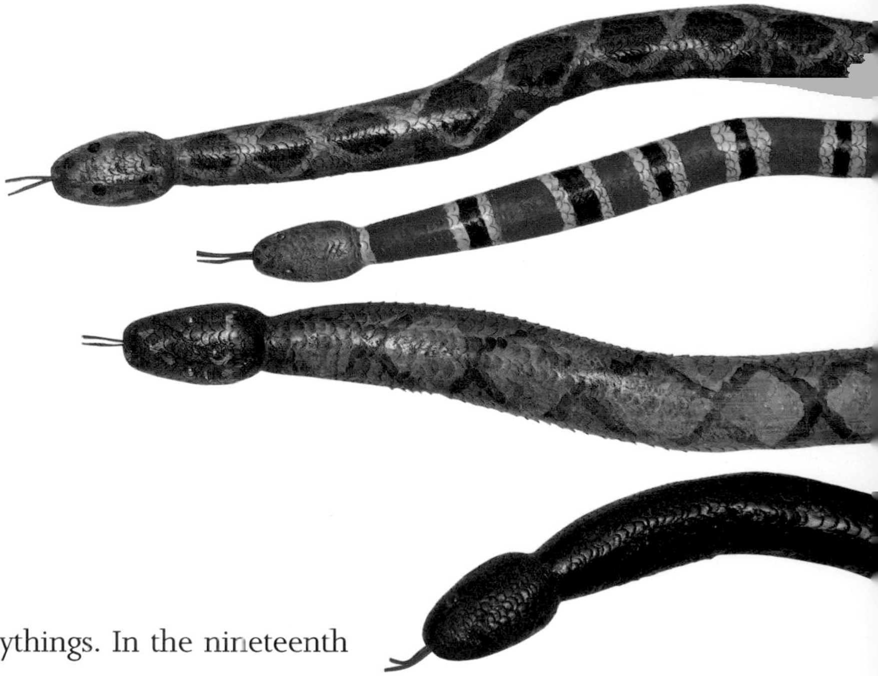

as outworkers to produce the elements of composite playthings. In the nineteenth century, dolls' houses became less precious, and were actually created with the object of amusing children. Paper manufacturers responded by producing replica wallpaper, miniature parquet and lino for floors, brickwork for the outside and even entire exteriors to be stuck on to board.

Queen Victoria disapproved of youthful idle hands, and presented her sons with a Swiss chalet in which they could learn carpentry with child-sized tools in a diminutive workshop. Industry was the lesson to be learned. The humbler Wendy House, soon filtered down to the masses, often consisting of just a couple of wobbly, hinged and painted boards with a door and window, and none the worse for that.

Today, wood is still venerated for its intrinsic and lasting beauty, which no amount of Day-Glo colour or wobbly bits can endow to plastic. Try your hand at making this painted wooden fish – time and energetic play will only improve its scaly contours, making it a fit toy to bequeath to your grandchildren.

Above left and right *A Carolina Blue Ridge snake carver, and a handful of his sibillant creations, complete with sinister forked tongues.*

Below *A much-loved hobby-horse, simply constructed from a sawn log of wood, branches and planks.*

NICOLA HENSHAW'S PULL-ALONG FISH

Left Nicola's bestiary: a wickedly grinning crocodile, a flock of well-fed seabirds, a frog prince, and a gloomy tortoise strangely transmuted into a salad bowl. A striped version of our fish keeps a wary eye out for passing gannets.

Right Forming a shoal on the sand, frog, feather and fin display their finer points, while the crocodile snacks on a flat-fish. Skill, imagination and ingenuity characterize Nicola's work, which is brought to life by her subtle sense of colour and robust humour.

Nicola Henshaw's robust, jokey menagerie is the distillation of a lifetime's fascination with animals. From a youthful fondness for a friendly chameleon in Zimbabwe, to the admirable discipline of chilly drawing trips to the zoo and Birdworld in Farnham, Surrey, Nicola has always relished the particular and peculiar behaviour of certain creatures; whether observing the precise post-prandial waddle of the alligator, or noting the exact deportment of the puffin. And if Edward Lear or Lewis Carroll happened to write a limerick extolling the pelican whose bill holds more than his belly can, or gently smiling all-embracing crocodile jaws, so much the better. The stories of Aesop, Kipling and Roald Dahl, as well as lively moral fables from her three years in Africa, have all served as inspiration for her quirky imagination, and a close look at many of her animals will reveal some hidden idiosyncracy: the pink flamingo with a crop full of fish, or the self-satisfied seagull full of starfish, shells, and sea-horses. Her rocking elephants, duck, frog and tortoise tables, and leopard storage boxes are undeniably furniture, though probably not the most likely product of an alumnus of an art college's Furniture for Industry course. Nicola exhibits her work all over the country, and it is quickly snapped up, particularly by eager Belgian and Japanese collectors. Her chunky spotted fish is a great opportunity for you to profit from all her hard work and acquire a witty and distinctive Henshaw lookalike in return for a few afternoons of therapeutic whittling, painting and gluing.

PROJECT: *NICOLA HENSHAW'S PULL-ALONG FISH*

Simple and decorative fun, this wooden toy is custom-made for a fish-friendly child. To make Nicola's trundling fish you will need:

Materials

- 60 cm (24 in) of pine, 2.5 cm (1 in) thick and 12.5 (5 in) wide
- 45 cm (18 in) of beech ply, 6 mm (¼ in) thick and 12.5 cm (5 in) wide
- 15 cm (6 in) of 6 mm (¼ in) dowelling
- 3 mm (⅛ in) metal rod or nail

Tools

- Jigsaw
- Drill and 6 mm (¼ in) drill bit
- 3 mm (⅛ in) drill bit for tail hinge
- 6 cm (2½ in) saw drill bit for wheels
- Chisel
- Paper, pencil and scissors
- Wood glue
- Water-based transparent inks and watercolours
- Varnish or wax (Antiquax or Bri-wax)
- Sandpaper and wire wool
- Bench vice
- Compass

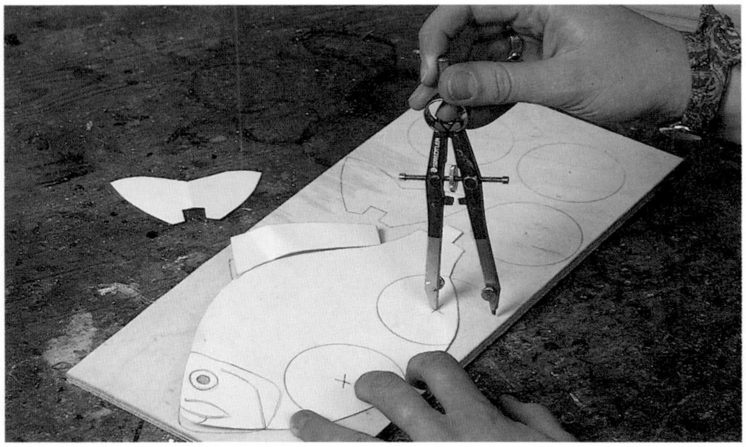

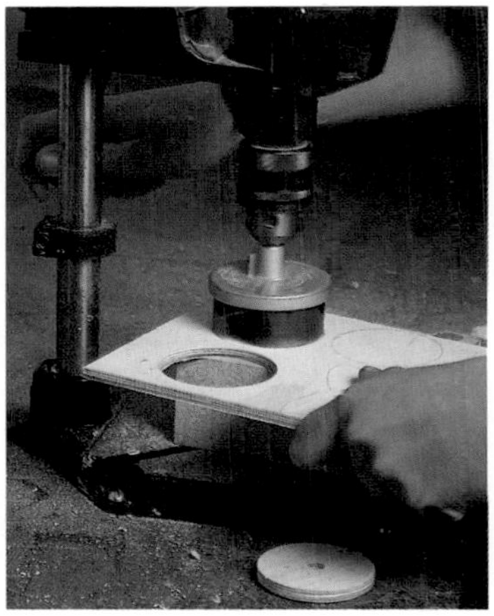

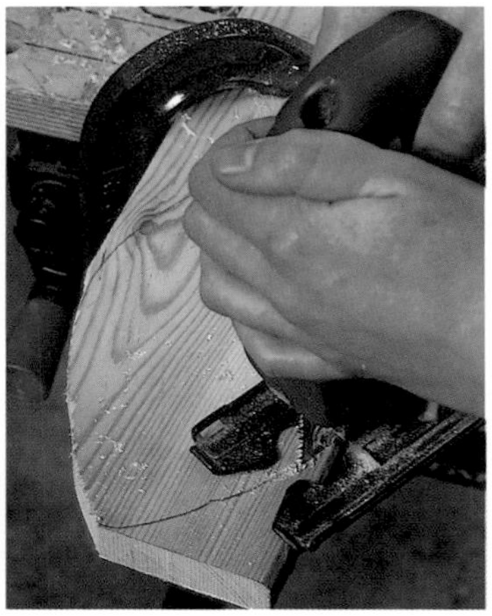

1 Draw the fish on paper, using the drawing overleaf as a guide and cut out to use as a template. Draw around template on to plywood, making holes for wheel axles. Draw tail, fin, and 3×6 cm (2½ in) diameter wheels.

2 Cut wheels using a 6 cm (2½ in) saw drill bit.

3 Draw and cut 2 identical fish shapes from the 2.5 cm (1 in) thick pine. Cut out plywood shapes using a jigsaw.

4 Carefully drill a hole through the pine shapes for the back axle. Then, using a jigsaw, cut a semi-circular hole in the plywood which will house the back wheel.

5 Drill a hole through the plywood fish and tail for the hinge. Use a metal rod or long nail to attach the tail, leaving it free to move from side to side.

6 Insert the dowelling rod for the back wheel axle. Sand the back wheel so that it moves freely. Glue the 3 fish layers together and drill a hole for the front wheel axle.

7 Secure the fish to the bench vice to hold it steady and roughly carve with a chisel. Try to taper the sides so that the tail and head end are flatter than the middle.

8 Bring the fish to life by carefully picking out the details of gills, face and fins with the chisel on both sides.

9 Paint with undiluted ink or liquid watercolour, building up subtle shading and a rich variety of tone with layers of different colour.

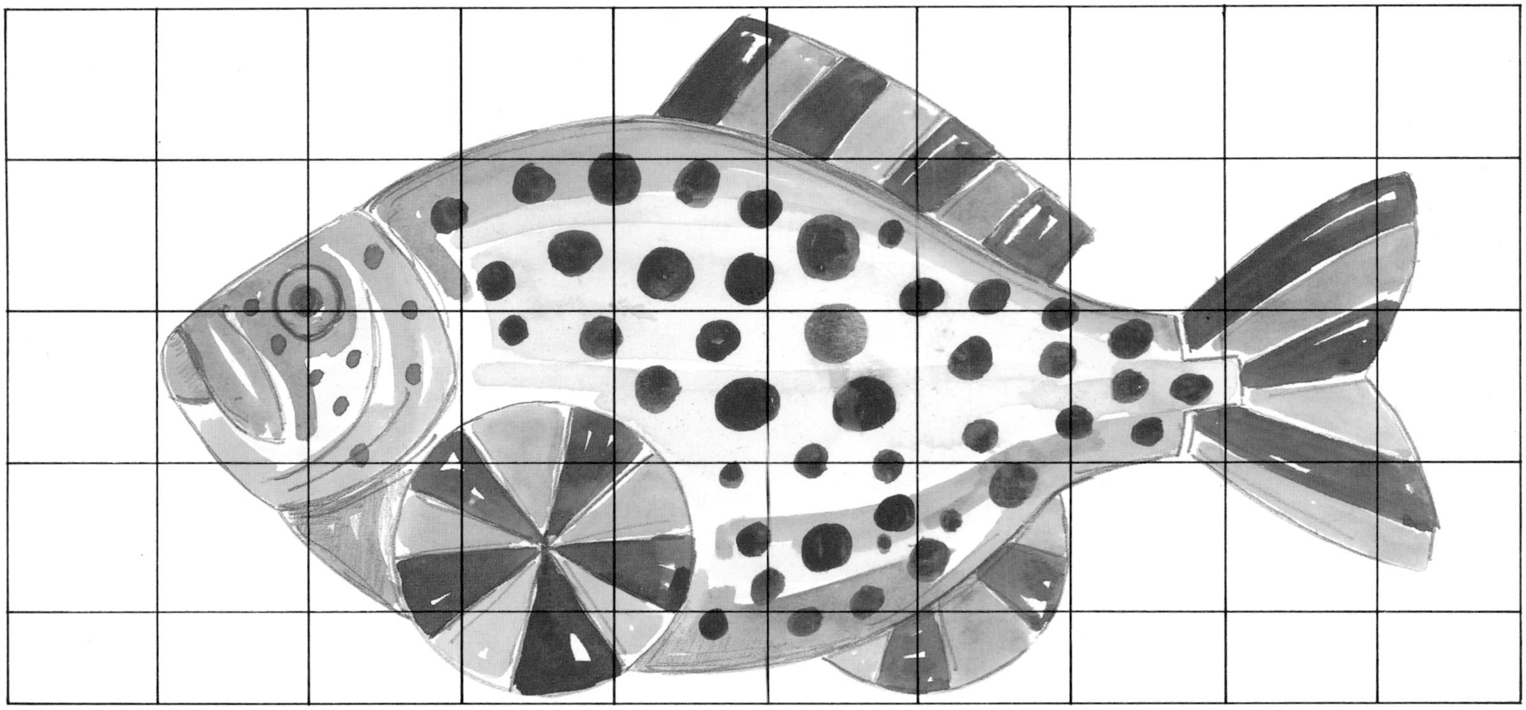

10 Use sandpaper and wire wool to knock back the colour, and to blend and soften the paint finish. Attach the front wheels using the remaining dowelling. A coat of wax or varnish will seal in and intensify the colour, giving a smooth and tactile feel.

Above *A scaled-down version of the spotted fish, showing its simple articulated tail, wheel positions, and the details of its fins, lips, gills and glassy eyes. To enlarge the template, either cheat and use an enlarging photocopier or projector (on 160%), or draw up a grid of the same number of squares but make each one 3 cm (1¼ in). Transfer the fish freehand to your new grid. Your final fish should measure approximately 26.5 cm (10½ in) from nose to tail.*

WEATHERVANES

Below *A weathered wooden rooster, of faded indigo and Venetian red, whose tail may have been used for target practice in some lawless past age. It is now under the protection of the Shelburne Museum.*

Right *Two exuberant whirligig figures, ready to wave frantic spoon and fork once they find their proper home on the pinnacle of the barn roof.*

Far right *A flashing, gilded, three-dimensional metal cockerel, grounded in a sympathetic roosting place.*

The state of wind and weather have always been important to the farmers who made their living from the land and the sailors to whom the sea was master. The word itself derives from a Danish or German word for a small flag and in the beginning most weathervanes were shaped like a fluttering pennant. While the wealthy could afford the cunning innovation of connecting the vane on the roof to a dial on an indoor ceiling, those who could not aspire to such dizzy reaches of high technology had to go out and brave the blizzards to check their humble weathervane and see which way the wind was blowing.

Weathervanes have been around since classical times, the most famous, a bronze triton, having an appropriate place on the pinnacle of the Tower of the Winds built by Andronicus in Athens around 100 BC. They are recorded in Great Britain as early as 1300, known then as *veder-cocs*, and there is one depicted on top of the original Westminster Abbey in the Bayeux Tapestry of 1077. They made their first appearance in America in the seventeenth century, beginning with a copper cockerel that roosted above the Dutch Reformed Church at Albany in 1656 – in fact this signalled such prowess in the genre

Above *Twilight and matching moons, one metal and one NASA's secret formula.*

that Picasso once said: 'Cocks have always been seen, but never as well as in American weathervanes.'

Paul Revere, the eighteenth-century maestro of metal-work, had a copper codfish peppered with copper nails on the roof of his workshop in Massachusetts. The first professional weathervane maker was one 'Deacon' Shem Drowne, born in 1683, who made a weathervane for the old province house in Boston which was later described as: 'An Indian chief, gilded all over . . . bedazzling the eyes of those who looked upward, like an angel in the sun.'

Weathervanes were used to announce religion with fish, golden roosters – both ancient religious symbols – or the Archangel Gabriel blowing his trumpet on church eaves; or to advertise trade with such devices as a gloved hand, a pipe, farming livestock, pheasants or dolphins. Farmers were likely to deck their rooftops with fat cattle, leaping stags or prancing horses; sailors favoured wheeling gulls, serpents, mermaids, ships, whales or fish. Weathervanes could also draw attention to political correctness – in eastern Pennsylvania the prevalent Indian perennially drawing his bow on the eaves of settlers' homes was intended to indicate to any other Indians in the vicinity that the land had been fairly bought and paid for. A semi-mythical Delaware Indian chief was eventually canonized as Saint Tammany for his eloquence and courage, and soon became reincarnated as an august weathervane above a lodge building in East Branch, New York, belonging to the Improved Order of Redmen. His body, perforated with bullet holes, attests not to some local battle, but to the predilection of passing dudes to target practice.

In America, patriotism prevailed at rooftop level, and the skyline was punctuated by a host of eagles, Uncle Sams, Columbias and Liberties. Elsewhere weathervanes were an unlikely means of settling scores: for the Duc de Choiseul, having the metal profile of his old enemy Voltaire face about to every passing blast was the next best thing to having his head on a pike.

Above *Copper, veiled with verdigris, with a yacht becalmed and bowing to no breeze. Verdigris is easy to replicate, and is guaranteed to bestow an air of venerable dignity on the most mundane object.*

Weathervanes were made of professionally cast metal or hand-carved wood, often gracefully sculptural and with an exaggerated silhouette, designed to show up to advantage from a distance. For the same reason bright colours and gilding which flashed in the sunlight were used. Iron, zinc and copper were usually left bare, but where wood was used, paint – usually solid white or Indian red – protected it from the elements. Cheapskates faked gilding with yellow ochre, while the likes of Inigo Jones and Sir Christopher Wren (whose creation was a nine foot long dragon) had vanes made from gilded beaten copper with wrought iron compass points. Sir Thomas Gresham immortalized his family coat of arms with an eleven foot grasshopper that pirouettes above the Royal Exchange, doubtless indicating the financial fluctuations within. American weathervanes, by contrast, have been said to display 'a heraldry of democracy'.

Most weathervanes were more humble, carved at home from pine, sanded and painted. They served their purpose, often with wit and charm, and were a source of pride to their makers, although they did not last forever. They are a happy tradition, and one which should be revived, despite our reliance on the Meteorological Office for its crisp yet dull proclamations.

Right Fox, fish and feathers in a multicoloured congregation, demonstrating a thrilling sizzle of paint partnerships that is easily achieved. Forget the terminal tedium of sanding, filling and finicky finishing; in some cases a fine nonchalance is the most effective approach, exploiting the quirks and character of bare timber.

CHRIS *M*OWE'S *F*OXY *W*EATHERVANE

Chris Mowe is an antique dealer with a penchant for countrified, naïve objects. But, faced with a shortage of genuine wind-battered weathervanes, he has taken matters into his own hands, and he makes his own. One of the many charms of old decorative country pieces is that they were originally constructed with the simplest of tools and the merest lick of paint. The appeal lies not in the skill of the maker as much as his or her wit, ability to caricature, enjoyment of colour and general sense of fun. Making such pieces is not reliant on fine art or skills, or even woodworking expertise, it is just a colourful whim and a chance to exercise your creative muscles.

Chris makes no great claims for the weathervanes and Shaker-style peg-rails that he sells: 'Whatever I do is naïve – I'm not gifted with any figurative talent. I just make things that appeal to me.' He also produces traditional paints and brushes because he couldn't buy them anywhere: 'A lot of the old cupboard interiors were finished in milk paint. I got casein [milk protein used for soft paint colours] and learned how to make paint to produce the same effect – originally the journeyman painters had to make do with what they found, dairy products, skimmed milk.' Mixing up old-fashioned paint is not quite as simple as he makes out, and while the main ingredient may be nothing more esoteric than powdered coffee whitener, the hydrochloric acid, ammonia and pigments tend to be found further afield than the store-cupboard.

He is a touch disingenuous when he claims: 'You could just take skimmed milk and crush a blackberry in it, or add onion skins, brick dust or yellow clay, and paint with it.' However, his own paints work, and the colours have the magic property of natural and earth pigments. They all marry beautifully with each other, giving a mellow effect that can be sanded easily to look worn. They also adhere to bare wood without primers and fillers, so that the character of the wood remains; they do not form a skin like modern emulsions; and the whole painted object can be further aged and embellished by using pigmented wax as a sealer.

Much of his inspiration comes from America, Germany, Holland and Scandinavia: 'I like Shaker furniture – it's uncomplicated and easy to live with. It shows the way they lived and worked. The straightforward cleanness of it and the quality of its production is the appeal.'

Above Chris at work on a brilliant fish: the templates on the walls bear witness to an enduring fondness for American folk art, and the range of hand-mixed paint reveals a familiarity with traditional finishes and colours.

He also has an unexpected passion for making Japanese marbled paper: 'They use it almost like meditation. They believe that whatever you feel comes out on the paper.' Frustrated that the raw materials were so hard to come by, he started to collect his own, including seaweed and ox-gall, in order to make special paints, water-based lacquers, sealers and stains. He extended his range to include scratch, brass and polishing brushes.

PROJECT: CHRIS MOWE'S FOXY WEATHERVANE

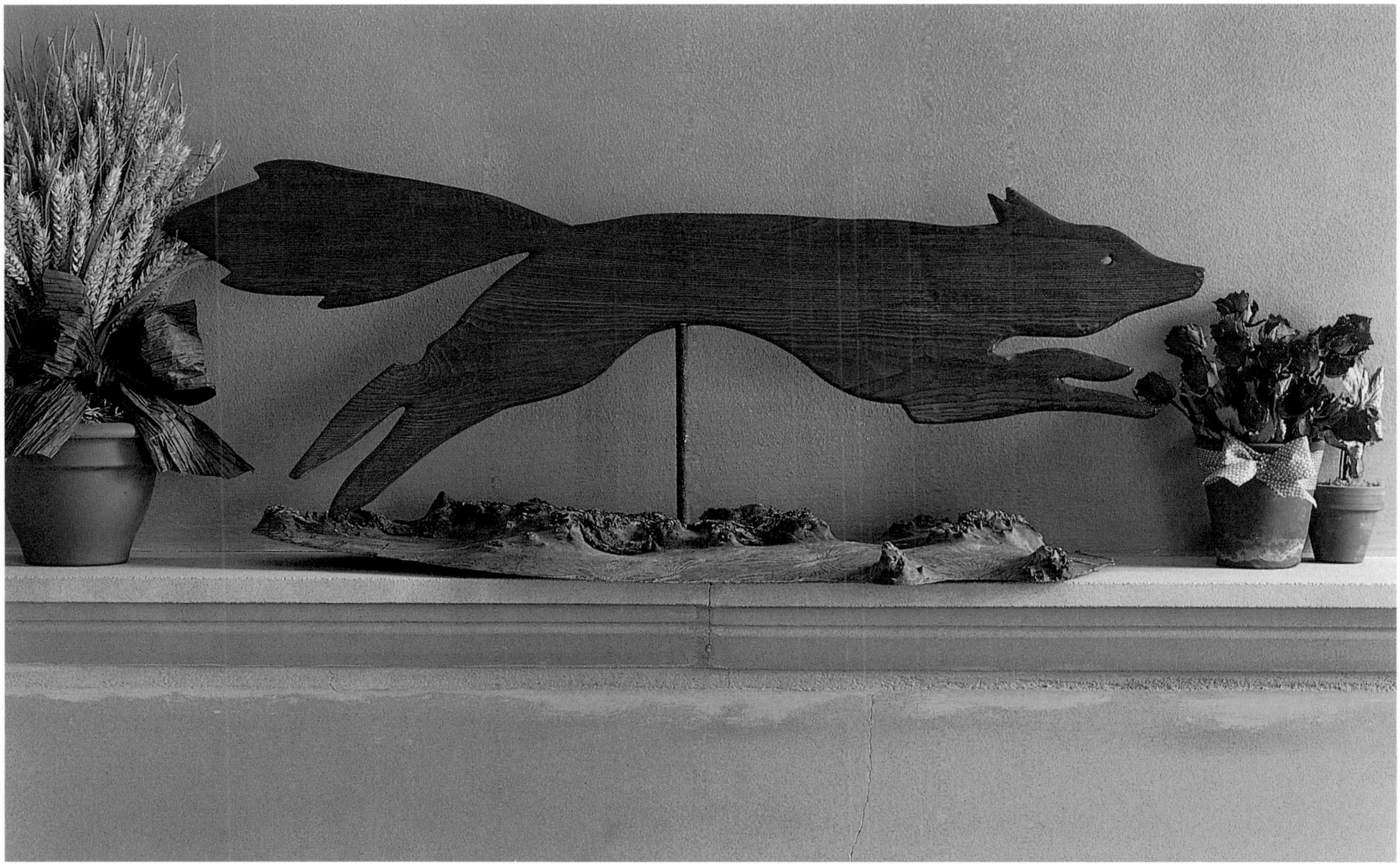

A sleek and wily fox to tell which way the wind blows, or simply as a russet reminder of the great outdoors.
To make Chris Mowe's foxy weathervane you will need:

Materials

- 30×82.5 cm (12×33 in) softwood plank 2.5 cm (1 in) thick
- 1cm (½ in) thick rusty metal rod for stand
- Shellac or proprietary sealer
- Water-based emulsion paints: red, ochre
- Wax or varnish
- Flat-bottomed piece of driftwood for base or if used as weathervane 1 cm (½ in) diameter brass tube and ball bearing

Tools

- Pencil and graph paper
- Bandsaw or jigsaw
- Drill
- Rasp
- Blow-torch
- Brass brush
- Sponge
- Sandpaper

1 Use photograph above to make a template. Use graph paper or a photocopier to enlarge and trace around it on to wood.

2 Clamp the wood to the edge of the workbench for stability. Carefully cut around the outline of your fox template with a bandsaw or jigsaw. Drill a hole for the eye.

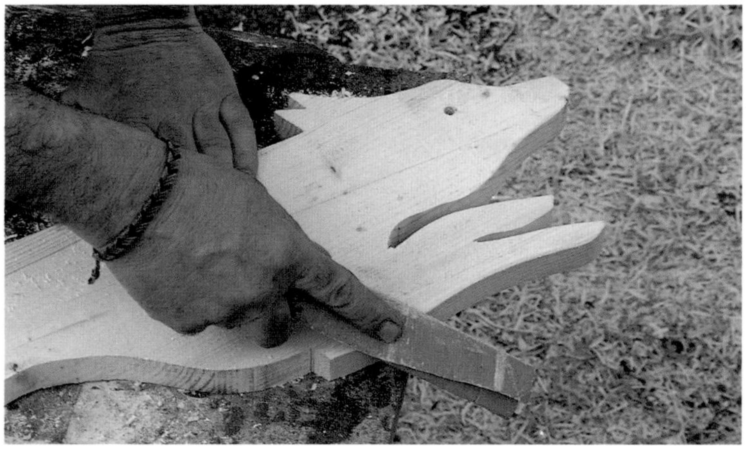

3 If there are any jagged edges, smooth and round off with a rasp or use a piece of sandpaper wrapped around a block of wood.

4 When the fox is sufficiently smooth, you can then weather it with a blow torch if desired. Scorch the entire fox on both sides using a blow torch.

5 Brush out burnt wood with brass brush to bring out grain and give it a weathered look. Leave wood brown. Seal with thin shellac, or any sealer.

6 With a wet sponge apply a thin coat of water-based ochre paint. Allow this to dry thoroughly before applying the next layer of paint.

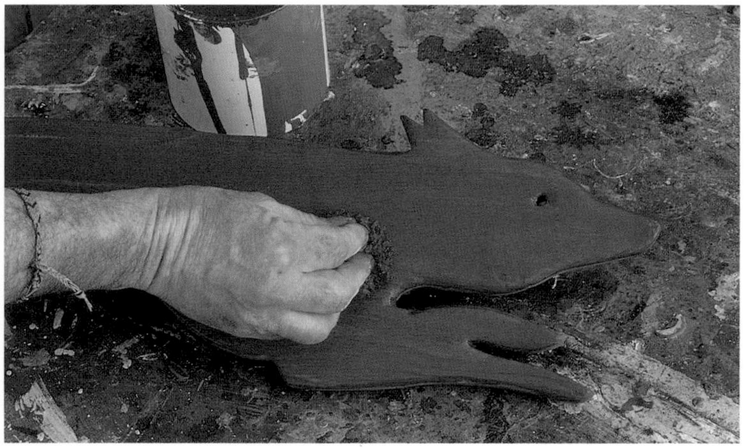

7 Add a thin layer of foxy red paint with a wet sponge, allowing ochre colour to show through slightly.

8 Sand gently. Seal with varnish, or if the weathervane is for indoors, shellac or wax. Drill 1 cm (½ in) hole in the base of the fox and in driftwood base. Stand fox in driftwood with metal rod. For use as a weathervane, drill hole in fox as before and insert 1cm (½in) brass tube to take metal rod, carefully placed towards the front of fox. Stand metal rod in brass tube with ball bearing at the bottom.

GAMEBOARDS

Gameboards evolved from the simplest of geometric designs scratched in the dust by primitive tribesmen with a mind to while away the time. A handful of the oldest games include *Parcheesi* which comes from India and derives from the Hindi word *pachis* meaning twenty-five, which itself evolved from the Korean game, *Nyout*. This, in turn, became the parent of Ludo; *Hyena* played by the Baggara Arabs of the Sudan; and *Mancala*, which comes from Africa – all consist of patterns which could easily be traced in the sand, and incorporate playing pieces of wood, ivory, pebbles or shells. The Indians of North America played a precursor of draughts, called Fighting Serpents.

Among more familiar board games, something like the games of Goose, and Snakes and Ladders were entombed with Egyptians of 2500–5000 BC to amuse them in the afterworld. The Greeks played something similar, but the *Guioco dell'Oca* (The Game of Goose) in its modern form is ascribed to Francisco de' Medici in the sixteenth century. The Duchess of Norfolk enjoyed it so much that she had a hornbeam version planted in her Worksop garden. The Chinese exercised their minds with *Wei-ch'i* (also known as Go) three millenia ago, and which is still challenging today. Chess was invented in the Orient over one thousand years ago. In eighth-century Japan a similar game called *Shogi* began to tax the minds of the intelligentsia. Ringo has an unusual circular board and originated in Germany; Queen's Guard is similar with a board marked out in hexagons; Fox and Geese found its way from Scandinavia in the Middle Ages to broaden the European games repertoire from a diet of draughts (which Penelope's suitors used to play as she worked on her tapestry), backgammon (*Duodecim Scripta* to the Romans), and Nine Men's Morris.

Above *A twentieth-century pastiche of a quaint old-fashioned draughts-board with crackled paint, stencilled squares, and scenes from the rural good life depicted top and bottom.* Far right *An unusual circular backgammon board, displaying just about every sophisticated paint technique known around the points of the compass.*

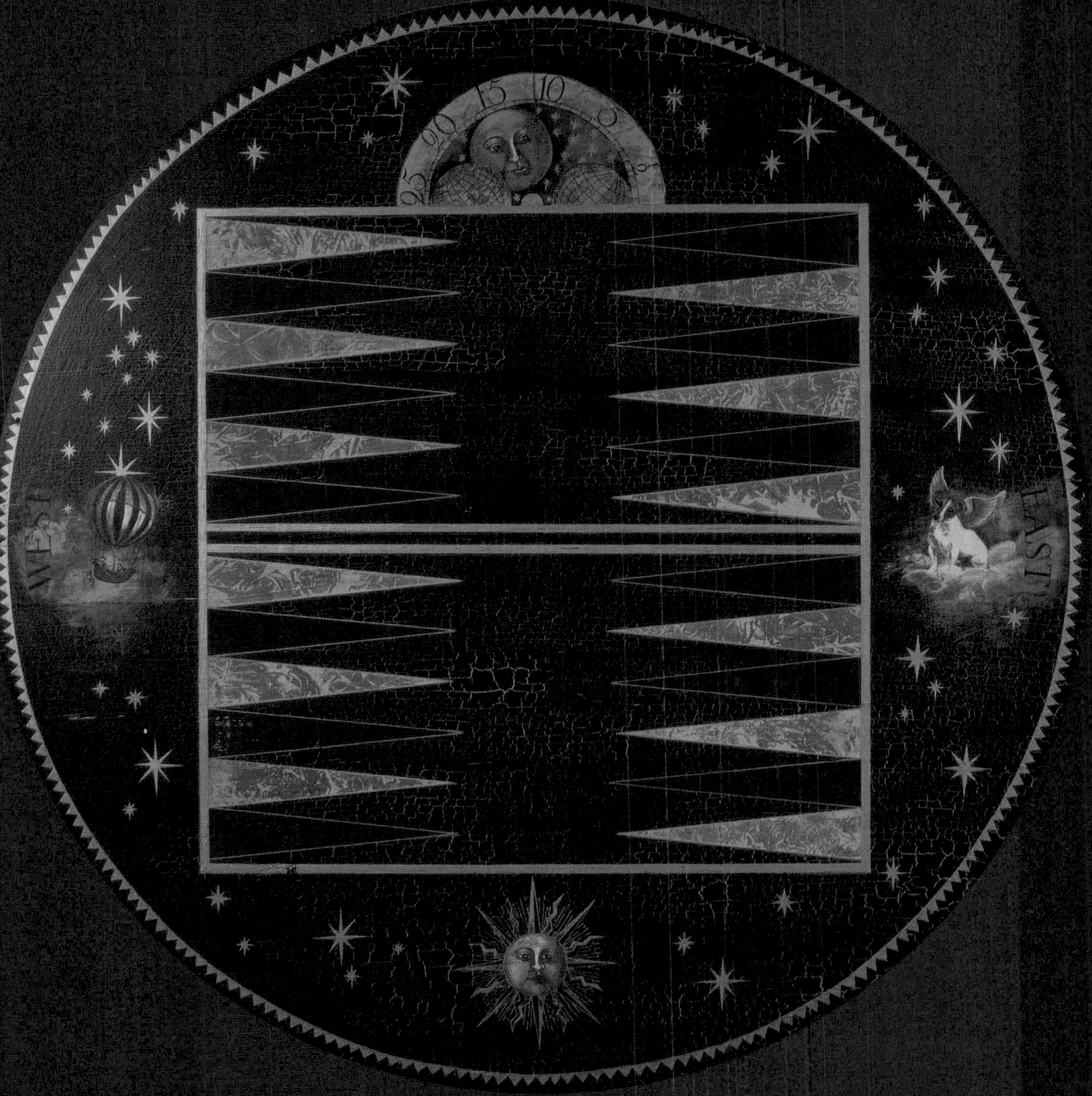
25 20 15 10 5
WEST
EAST

Above top *A Rococo draughtsboard by Sara Delafield Cook, the height of sophistication in sober gold and black craquelure.*

Above *Same technique, same colours in a rather more light-hearted gameboard by Fiona Denholm, quietly embellished by date and monogram and elegant freehand border.*

Right *A bone-simple house in the Hamptons, unadorned save for a pair of decoy swans and an immaculately plain gameboard.*

Games are both a diversion from, and a rehearsal for, the serious business of life – in the unpredictable combinations of luck and skill which the player brings, in the grace with which he can lose or win, in the obsession, the need to cheat, to win at all costs, the inheritance lost on the throw of dice. Most games parallel a sense of powerlessness with the feeling that if we just pay lip service to a particular superstition, try this combination of moves, or that logical approach, good fortune will soon follow.

Both scientists and poets have uses for the game as an analogy for life. The 'Theory of Games' was a matter of some excitement to the mid-twentieth-century economists John von Neumann and Oskar Morgenstern who used it as a model for competitive economic behaviour. Previously, games were seen as more spiritually enlightening – the Victorian biologist T. H. Huxley put it thus: 'The chess-board is the world; the pieces are the phenomena of the universe; the rules of the game are what we call the laws of Nature. The player on the other side is hidden from us. We know that his play is always fair, just, and patient. But we also know, to our cost, that he never overlooks a mistake, or makes the smallest allowance for ignorance.'

Shakespeare made the game a symbol of cosmic order, and when things were not going well between Oberon and Titania in *A Midsummer Night's Dream*, among other disasters, the fact that 'The nine men's morris is filled up with mud', portended no good. Shakespeare was alluding to the way that shepherds would pass their time, using stones and a diagram cut into the turf. But it was the little-known author, Grantland Rice (1880–1954), of an unfamiliar work, *Alumnus Football*, who elevated the idea into the platitude we know and love:

'For when the One Great Scorer comes
To write against your name,
He marks – not that you won or lost –
But how you played the game.'

Above *A tribute to the decorative power of a chequered board. Transitory Christmas paraphernalia aside, this tastefully bare hall would be utterly empty without its carefully placed square of toning greens and browns.*

SUE MARTIN'S CHEQUERED GAMEBOARD

Far left *Gambolling lambs, frolicking foals, ponderous penguins and prancing piglets; Sue Martin's fondness for animals is apparent on her gameboards, in their attitudes of cheerfully sentimental exuberance.* Left *A vision of utter, pleasurable absorption; to Sue Martin the making of gameboards is as much fun as any game. There is nothing to equal the glow of achievement on planning, painting and completing something so dramatic, simple and quick to make. For animal reference, loiter around a pigsty, or rootle in the comfort of your local library for animal picture books.*

Animals are Sue Martin's passion: 'I'm an animal addict – I have two dogs, a cat and three guinea pigs. My mother has three old horses and a burro. We used to have a goat farm too.' She is a member of various ecological groups, and the penguins and polar bears that disport themselves on her gameboards reflect the concern she feels for their natural habitat.

She has long collected folk art, and did not give a thought to gameboards, until she attended an auction at which a gameboard came up for sale. She fell in love with it and bid, but not enough: 'I had to have it. It was a great example of folk art with bears on it. Of course, when the bidding went way over my budget, I was very disappointed. So I went home and painted one just like it.' So began a very lucrative business.

She lives in the Hudson Valley, which she describes as: 'A little like stepping back in history. In the winter nobody talks to anybody round here – when the snow is up to my thighs I don't go anywhere. You don't visit. You have to dig your way out. I wouldn't trade it for anything.' Winter and summer, she works a seven-day week making animal gameboards. Rabbits were traditionally a sign of good luck in pioneer days, and she uses a rabbit motif from old Chinese wallpaper amongst her designs. Pigs, thought to bring good luck in Germany, also make an appearance, and her backgammon boards are generally decorated with horses. And when the prospect of making endless gameboards palls, she turns her hand to other things, from tiny boxes to painted dower chests, bringing them all to life with her peaceable kingdom of animals.

PROJECT: SUE MARTIN'S CHEQUERED GAMEBOARD

Spotted pigs prancing in a flowery meadow, what better image to assuage the pangs of losing or temper triumph at winning? To make Sue Martin's chequered gameboard you will need:

Materials

- 40×60 cm (16×24 in) piece of birch or maple
- Stylus or pen
- Off-white and black acrylic paint
- 2 oz each burnt umber, peachy pink, pink, 3 different greens for grass, yellow and flower colours acrylic paints
- White graphite paper
- 2.15 m (7 ft) fine wooden beading
- Woodstain: walnut and cherry mixed
- Wood glue
- 1 cm (½ in) nails
- Varnish

Tools

- Brushes
- Sandpaper
- Ruler and pencil
- Saw
- Hammer

The 7 pig shapes that you will need to trace on to your board.

1 Paint board off-white. Sand lightly if necessary and give a second coat. Measure borders 10 cm (4 in) at each end and paint them black. Draw a 5 cm (2 in) square grid on board and paint alternate squares black.

2 Paint green grass on the black borders with light one-directional strokes, using different greens and the occasional touch of brown. Draw pigs using the templates opposite and trace on to the board using graphite paper.

3 Paint pigs with features and pink-brown hoofs. With a stylus or old pen, dot white stars in the sky and paint a moon. Add wildflowers if you wish. For more grass use a scruffy brush.

4 Sand the whole board lightly with fine sandpaper. Cut 2 lengths of beading each for sides, ends and dividers to fit. Stain and sand to make them look worn. Glue and nail stained wood pieces. Sand lightly to smooth and touch up any gaps in paint or stain. Varnish.

Automata

Play is one of the most precious attributes of civilization. Pre-Columbian children amused themselves by dragging clay animals around on wheels – no mean achievement since in Mexico at the time the wheel had not actually been invented. As early as 200 BC engineers and mechanics, Hero of Alexandria among them, were scratching their heads and creating Heath Robinson-like devices powered by water and steam to make fake birds sing, Hercules slay hissing dragons, and temple doors mysteriously spring open. The Chinese put more power and 'oomph' into their automata, using gunpowder to fuel their moving toys, occasionally propelling their maker further and faster than he desired.

In Germany, there has been a strong tradition for hand-carved wooden toys since the Middle Ages, and until the nineteenth century, toy-makers' guilds were a powerful force with the same kind of protective function as present-day unions. The familiar wooden pecking hens, Jacob's ladders and tumbling acrobats come with a pedigree of several hundred years refined and simplified over time.

As clocks and clockwork became more sophisticated, so also did mechanical toys, which exploited the properties of balance and counter-balance, weights, cams, levers, magnetism, centrifugal force, swings, wheels, pendulums and springs, among other ingenious devices. By the end of the seventeenth century, the Swiss had established their pre-eminence in such matters, and were turning out exquisite miniature musical boxes; the much-maligned cuckoo clock was just one facet of a whole range of mechanical masterpieces. By the early nineteenth century, Louis Rochat

Left *A slithering dragon on a pole, all arms and legs and serrated tail, with a dreamy and benign expression on his face.*

Right *A gaggle of carved and painted ducks, and a couple of ornothological unknowns, presided over by an enraged cockerel whirligig.*

Right *A wily and wicked fox fattens up his living larder. The figures were carved from lime wood by Edessia Aghajanian, painted with Plaka paints, and then varnished.*

whiled away the long snowbound winter evenings near Geneva by making such *tours de force* as his exotic and orientally garbed magician, all nodding head and rolling eyes, who played the shell game hiding changing objects under a pair of cups, while music played and silk roses bloomed. Definitely a toy for grown-ups, this intricate piece of fantasy was destined to be kept out of the reach of marauding children at all costs. The less frivolous citizens of Nuremberg had to glean what fun they could from such delights as the *Adoration of the Magi*, and *Death Striking the Hours*. In this macabre vein, Goethe tried to persuade his mother to buy a model guillotine for his son. She, however, is reputedly known to have resisted his pleas for such a revolutionary automaton for her grandchild.

Above *Two Nigerian ladies pounding millet, made by the same artist. The struts activate frenzied pestling.*

Such was the tenor of the eighteenth and nineteenth centuries. Automata became more and more complicated and tended to be playthings of the bored aristocracy. This was the era of exquisite French clockwork models (still using Swiss movements) of violin and piano players, and strutting peacocks. When the key was turned, bisque beauties powdered their noses, sniffled into handkerchiefs, drew portraits, danced to the castanets, attempted to catch butterflies, blew bubbles and smoked cheroots. For animal lovers, there was *le lapin mal élevé*, a life-sized rabbit that waggled its feet, ears and mouth, and then lifted its tail to drop a chocolate on the floor. The names of the creators – Pierre Jaquet-Droz, Decamps, Theroude, Lambert and Vichy – are legendary among toy collectors, robot designers and auction houses.

At the less rarefied end of the scale, Charles Dickens described the stock at

Above *A cruder and more complicated piece of work from West Virginia, celebrating the machine age in the form of a rugged steam engine and three craggy operatives.*

Tackleton the Toy Merchant's in *The Cricket on the Hearth*: 'hideous, hairy, red-eyed Jacks-in-Boxes . . . movable old ladies who darned stockings or carved pies . . . and demoniacal Tumblers who wouldn't lie down, and were perpetually flying forward, to stare infants out of countenance.' He neatly encapsulated the purpose of this shop of horrors which might have been painted by Hieronymus Bosch, as producing toys to pacify middle-class children: 'who had played with them, and found them out, and broken them, and gone to sleep.' The exasperated parents of today's children, as they scrabble beneath the sofa for the vital component that brings some battery-operated nightmare to life, may well mutter '*plus ça change*', as they step back and hear the fatal crunch of plastic underfoot.

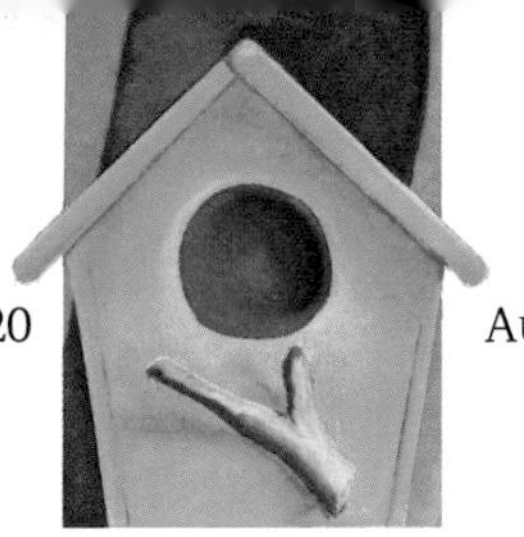

*J*OHN *M*ALTBY'S *S*EASIDE *A*UTOMATON

Left *Looking appropriately like an Old Salt, John Maltby adds the finishing touch of braid to one of his more theatrical pieces. Boats and bits of nautical paraphernalia sit becalmed among the birds and divas.*
Right *There is an air of British eccentricity about Maltby's automata, acting as light relief perhaps to his more serious ceramics. W.G. Grace, displaying full cricketing prowess, and the jauntiness of 'Hip Hip Hurrah', give evidence of an invincibly positive spirit. Maltby's light-hearted graphics and elegant lettering cheer the walls of the most discerning collectors.*

John Maltby is actually a sculptor and a potter and trained in the illustrious Leach ceramic tradition. He started by making the usual sets of plates, dishes and mugs, but rapidly concluded that a production line was boring. He has been a well-respected and individual potter for the last 25 years, making one-off, hand-decorated, very English-looking dishes. Intense spells of potting were broken by making presents for his wife of little bouncing wooden models of her in her 2CV car, or boats in craggy harbours overlooked by Bethesda Chapels: 'I'm so mean that I won't buy Christmas presents, I make them. The boats are really a way of relaxing after working for pottery exhibitions – they recharge my batteries.' The Maltbys are fond of naïve toys, whether Pakistani tigers or nodding animals from Japan, and have collected them from all over the world. John is also a collector of the boats and circus animals created by the late Sam Smith, a local eccentric whose satirical work is now much prized. The bold unpretentious influence of the painter Alfred Wallis is very evident in his little rocking boats in choppy Cornish waters. John's battery-charging antidote to his real work has taken on an unexpected importance and his Cornish vignettes grace some very discerning walls. As he freely admits: 'whenever we've tried to make a living, it's been disastrous, and whenever we haven't, it's been just a little less disastrous!'

Hip, Hip, Hurrah!
BRAVO! BRAVO!!

PROJECT: JOHN MALTBY'S SEASIDE AUTOMATON

Memories of childhood and a seaside souvenir – a little fishing-boat rocked by ocean waves. To make John's rocking boat you will need:

Materials

- Piece of 3 mm (1/8 in) thick plywood, 50×40 cm (20×16 in)
- White water-based emulsion
- Acrylic paints
- 2 cm (3/4 in) screws
- Pebble with a hole, fishing weight, or ceramic equivalent
- Strong wire
- 2×12.5 cm (5 in) lengths 2.5 cm (1 in) square section batten
- 2 wood blocks 3.5×1×5 cm (1½×½×2 in)
- Wood glue
- Piece of 1.5 cm (5/8 in) thick wood for boat, 7.5×5 cm (3×2 in)
- 2×3.5 cm (1½ in) lengths of 4.5 mm (3/16 in) dowel for masts
- Matchsticks for cross-trees
- Semi-matt varnish
- Cardboard or thin Formica for sails
- Stapler

Tools

- Saw
- Sandpaper
- Drill and 1.5 mm (1/16 in) drill bit
- Screwdriver
- Pliers
- Cardboard comb for texturing paint

1 Cut a piece of plywood 25×30 cm (10×12 in) in size, and cut top in curve. Sand edges and glue 2 battens to reverse side. Cut a front piece 25×10 cm (10×4 in) and glue 2 blocks of wood as shown.

2 When dry, paint both pieces with white emulsion or undercoat. When dry, paint background blue-grey and run a cardboard 'comb' over wet paint to make waves. For the sky, flick on a lighter colour.

3 Mix in additional colours as you please to give a richer finish. Paint in landscape, islands, houses and lighthouse with acrylic paint, leaving the central area free to accommodate the boat.

4 Cut out boat and sandpaper to taper at front. Paint with undercoat and acrylics. Drill holes for cross-trees in dowels, and for dowels in base of boat, angled slightly backwards. Glue together. Cut sails. Glue to back.

Right *Push the wire up from the base to the back of the boat and staple in position.*

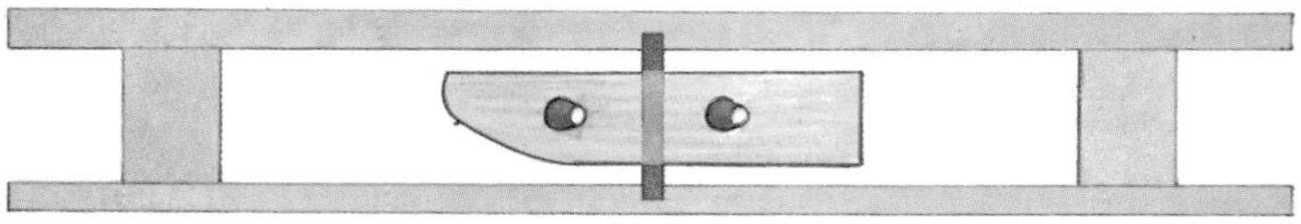

Below *An aerial view of the boat showing the central wire attaching the boat to the board.*

5 Drill a hole upwards through the underside from base to back of boat, and push a piece of wire up through it. Staple in place. Drill a small hole across the middle of boat for a wire balance. Place front piece on back piece and mark a point midway across on both pieces. Line up the points on the back of the front piece and the front of the back piece, and drill midway into the surface of the wood to hold the wire fulcrum of the boat. Attach the boat by sandwiching it between front and back with a piece of wire going from the base board hole through the body of the boat and into the hole at the back of the front board.

6 Screw front and back together from the back into the blocks, thereby fixing all the pieces together. Attach weight to wire at bottom of boat so that it swings. Apply a coat of semi-matt varnish.

*A*NIMAL *H*OUSES

Long ago, only the most useful of animals could aspire to man-made housing. They had to provide transport, eggs, milk, meat, or play an essential part in the hunt for food. Thus cow-byres were an integral part of medieval houses; handsome arched brick stables in lieu of up-and-over garages flanked many a Georgian villa; dovecotes, whose inhabitants provided meat in the dark days of winter, graced Elizabethan manors. The notion of keeping tame doves or pigeons for food probably originated in the Middle East at least 4000 years ago, and was adopted by the Romans who kept the birds in columbaria.

More ephemeral constructions of wood and wire protected chickens and rabbits from hungry foxes. Until the ancient forests started to be grubbed up for farmland in the seventeenth and eighteenth centuries, pigs were the roving responsibility of a swineherd, and foraged free among the brushwood. Pigsties are a comparatively newfangled invention.

Game hunting hounds, sporting-dogs and even the occasional house-dog had bijou residences from the fifteenth century onwards, and the remains of the dear deceased animals were later tearfully interred in canine mausoleums in many a grand park. One less Olympian means of housing was to use a wooden barrel on its side with a bed of straw as a kennel. The classic gable-roofed version can be

Above *An elegant abode for a dandy of the dog world, designed and built to commission for the rather more discerning hound.*

Right *A more humble chicken house: its sturdy legs keep out rising damp or rodents; the ramp can be managed by the most arthritic chicken; and the whole can be secured against foxes.*

Far right *A birdcage at Beckley Park, all gargoyles and beetling turrets, in which to keep your raven in gothic splendour.*

1749

dated back to at least the reign of Edward II, when the strange angular woman's head-dress seen on the queen in a pack of cards was given the name kennel. Presumably the habit of segregating hunting dogs behind bars came from Roman times, since the word kennel comes from the latin *canis.*

Gradually, people began to house more exotic creatures in their grounds. Peacocks, the glamorous iridescent natives of India, had to have a refuge from foxes and cold

Right *A bijou country cottage for fortunate small non-flying birds, whose reed-thatched roof is neatly framed by an arch of yew. Proof that you do not need to be amongst the landed gentry to keep a small flock of something feathered.*

weather, as did the budgerigars, zebra finches and canaries who twittered in airy wirework aviaries. Occasionally, some rich eccentric would need to find a home for a bear: at Killerton, in Devon, this consisted of a charming rustic building decorated throughout with twigs and pine-cones, with a floor of deer knuckles and a couple of small stained-glass windows. Mme de Pompadour commissioned a rather less enduring dwelling of brocade for her lap-dogs whilst in the eighteenth century Humphry Repton designed a lakeside chinoiserie dairy and a menagerie with one classical and one rustic façade for Woburn Abbey, and a magnificent trellis-work poultry house for a residence in Woodford. Unfortunately, very few of these buildings have survived, and little documentation remains.

There are a few commonsense rules to observe when embarking on the construction of a kennel, birdhouse, or bijou chalet for a cat (though cats, being cussed creatures, usually prefer to sit sulking on a window-sill in the rain, or to lurk unseen in the recesses of a paper bag, to enjoying the cosy charms of the shelter you lovingly create). Use weatherproof materials, and make sure that any paint or preservative is non-toxic. Allow sufficient ventilation for stifling summer days, and site away from the prevailing winter wind or rain direction. Make sure that you leave no nail points or sharp ends of wire sticking out. Make an overhanging roof and a raised solid floor to prevent the house from getting waterlogged. Allow space for food and water bowls, and arrange comfortable and disposable bedding. Birdhouse floors need to be accessible for cleaning and should be screwed, not glued in place, or new birds will look for more salubrious accommodation. Wrens are partial to a hanging birdhouse, swallows favour a solid wall or tree-mounted house, and robins like a simple roofed nesting shelf. They all prefer to be out of reach of your cat.

Above *An entire avian condominium, combining elements of American gothic, with onion domes courtesy of St. Basil's in Moscow. With a breathtaking view of the mountains on the Laniers' back-doorstep, any sensible bird would race to take up residence.*

Beyond this, let your architectural fantasies run riot and enjoy whatever folly comes to mind. The simple structure of kennels and birdhouses invites embellishment. They should be as much fun to make as dolls' houses, and much easier, with the additional advantage of providing shelter for grateful and entertaining inhabitants.

*B*ob and *C*harlotte *L*anier's *C*ottage *B*irdhouse

Bob and Charlotte Lanier seem to have discovered the secret of a happy life. Making things out of wood might not work for everyone, but it certainly does for them. Commander Lanier spent twenty-eight years in the Navy. He always enjoyed woodwork as a hobby, and Charlotte has had to cope with moving home more than twenty times during Bob's career: 'As a military wife, I developed the art of design out of necessity. Using what was to hand, and adding a lot of imagination I learned to create a warm and comfortable haven wherever we travelled.' So teaching herself to design, carve and paint the shelves, tables and whatnots she wanted came naturally.

Bob says: 'Once I left the military, she put me to work. Suddenly we had a tiger by the tail. We realized all of a sudden that we had a job that takes a ten-day week to complete . . . if we weren't having a good time, we wouldn't do it.' They have been building their strange and wonderful birdhouses and furniture for eight years now. When asked how many things they have made, Bob is apt to scratch his head: 'I reckoned sixty-seven different items . . . and that was without thinking about it too much.' He is currently puzzling out the logistics of a hanging cupboard in the form of a Noah's ark complete with a keel and animals.

Charlotte, who has a passion for antiques, describes what she wants, and Bob tries to make it. 'Neither one of us are real good draughtspeople. Eventually we get there.' Their shared pastime takes them all over the country, and they are invited to attend all the prestigious shows: 'If we get on each other's nerves, that's our fault. I just do what Charlotte tells me to do – we get along better that way. We've been married for forty-one years, and we're still trying to work out who's boss.' Woodwork may or may not be the secret of universal happiness, but judging by the Laniers who get on very well indeed, it is certainly worth a try. And at the very least, your local birds will be grateful for a bijou roof over their heads.

Far left *Giant Brobdingnags in a miniature birdhouse village, Bob and Charlotte Lanier have the perfect working relationship, enjoying the unpressurized fun of a hobby that has accidentally become something of a lucrative career.*

Above *Becomingly weathered in a glaucous grey-green, with its own weathervane and a handy entrance twig, the Lanier's simple birdhouse proffers an irresistible invitation to home-hunting birds.*

PROJECT: *BOB* AND *CHARLOTTE LANIER'S* COTTAGE *BIRDHOUSE*

A model of irresistible whimsy – a country retreat for a thrush family, complete with weathervane and twig perch.
To make Bob and Charlotte Lanier's country birdhouse you need:

Materials

- 20 cm×2.4 m (8 in×8 ft) pine board 1 cm (½ in) thick (not plywood)
- Waterproof wood glue
- Approx. 30×3 cm (1¼ in) finishing nails
- Latex acrylic paint
- Non-toxic acrylic polyurethane sealer
- Stain or raw umber to age
- Length of 3 mm (⅛ in) dowel
- Twig for perch

Tools

- Saw (table or sabre saws)
- Sandpaper
- Hammer
- Nail punch
- Paintbrush
- Drill and 3 mm (⅛ in) bit

1 Cut out eight pieces for the house to the sizes shown. Cut a 45 degree bevel on the top edge of the 2 sides to match the roofline. Assemble birdhouse as shown. All joints (except roof which should be removable for cleaning) should be glued as well as nailed for a tighter fit.

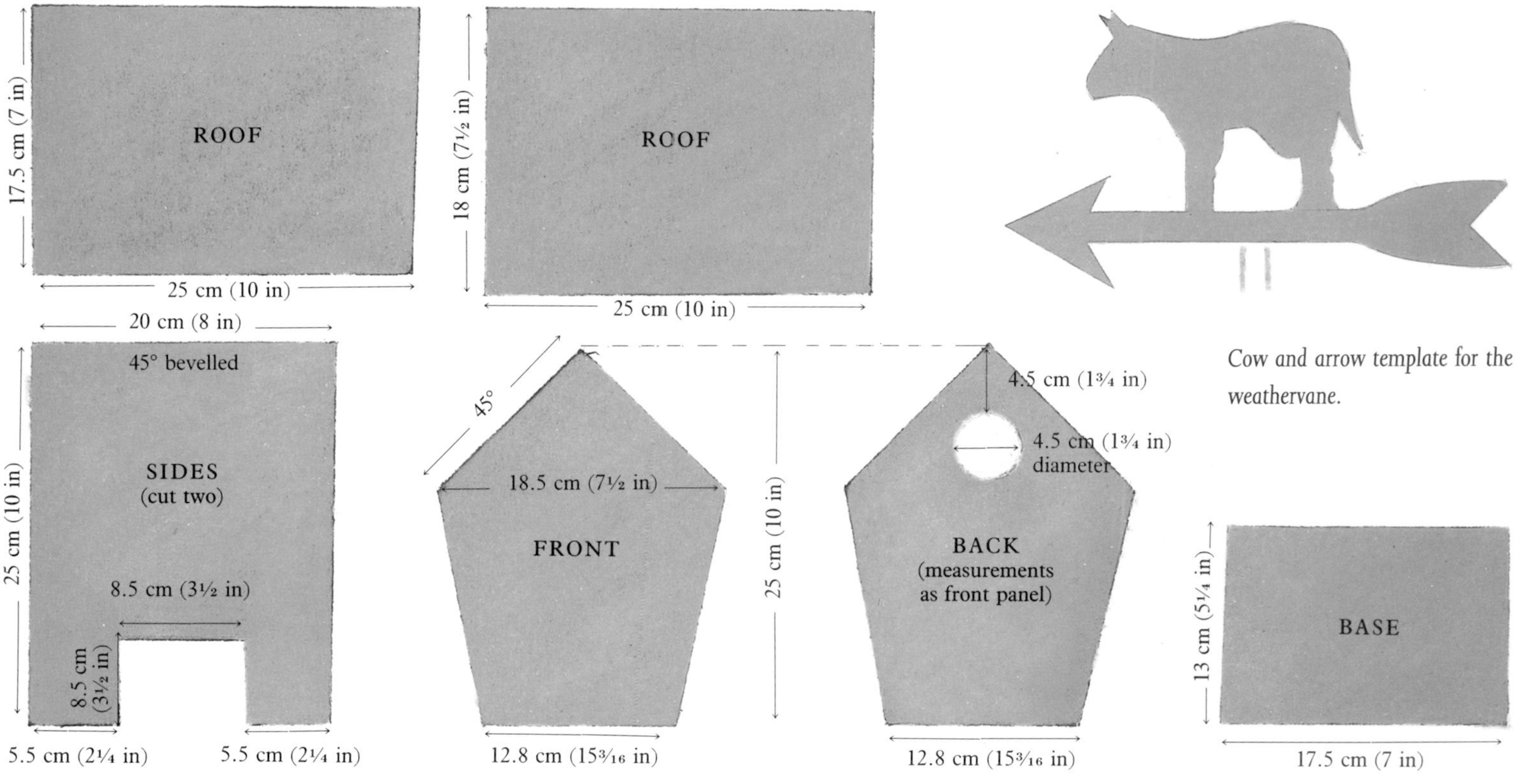

Cow and arrow template for the weathervane.

2 Butt the smaller roof piece against the apex, and place the larger on top. This should be screwed in place for ease of removal. Sand all joints and edges until smooth.

3 Paint with latex acrylic as desired. Allow to dry. Sand edges for a worn look. A stain or raw umber should be applied to the sanded parts. Seal to protect from the elements.

4 Using templates, mark and cut out cow and arrow separately. Sand edges and paint as you wish.

5 Carefully glue and pin cow to arrow. For a worn look, sand and apply a stain or raw umber as before.

6 Drill a 3 mm (1/8 in) hole in weathervane and apex of roof. Attach with a length of 3 mm (1/8 in) dowel. Nail chunky twig as perch to front just beneath entry hole.

*D*ECORATIVE *C*RAFT

By definition, decorative crafts are all the objects you don't need but like to have around. Nobody seriously needs a marbled paper and leather portfolio for their newspaper cuttings and you would probably not expire if your blanket chest was undecorated, but why settle for puritanical parsimony when spangled riches can be yours for the price of a pot of paint?

Above *A charming, hand-painted wall cupboard, crowned with fat sparrows.*
Right *Hand-painted plates reverberating with Mediterranean colours and sun-kissed blossoms.*

*P*AINTED CERAMICS

Potters today are moulding aeons of history between their fingers as they knead, and then pinch or coil the raw materials into a delicate bowl whose undulating lip betrays the hand of its maker. Since prehistoric man first chanced upon the potential of clay to take a shape and make a comely container, people have experimented with different ways of exploiting its texture, colour and malleability. The niceties of the Buddhist tea ceremony demand fine hand-shaped ceramics where the primitive conditions of their creation are tempered by the innate sophistication of the Japanese sense of style. The Chinese and Japanese were the first to exploit the decorative possibilities of clay, and it took centuries for the rest of the world to learn their secrets.

Above *A striking blue and cream marigold bowl enjoying pride of place on a country rush seat.*

Far right *Even simple zigzags and swirls look effective when executed in bright colours and deft brush strokes.*

From the Orient, the centre of activity moved to Islam, where an extraordinary transcendence of ceramic tiles dazzled the eyes of Mesopotamians from the ninth century AD onwards, with blue and green painted geometric and calligraphic motifs on brilliant white tin-glazed backgrounds. Tiles were further embellished with newly discovered iridescent lustre in rich ruby, brown and yellow. The effect was obtained by painting silver, copper or sulphur oxide on top of the ready-fired object.

In thirteenth-century Persia, Kashan potters increased the colour range by discovering cobalt and manganese, which produced a stable black and blue. They also developed enamel colours that were fixed by a second firing, a process known as *mina'i*. These two developments gave the Persian potters a repertoire of seven colours. Thus began the grand era of tile-making, during which an intricate kaleidoscope of

pattern was conferred on mosques and mihrabs (prayer-niches) from Samarkand to Seville. Arabic potters created a ceramic patchwork of squares, rectangles, hexagons, stars and crosses, further enriched with surface designs of dots, arabesques, calligraphy, plants, birds and animals. From Seville, the tradition for brilliant tile-clad buildings found its way to Mexico in the seventeenth century, and ebulliently bright church façades began to celebrate an extrovert deity in primary red, blue, yellow and green diamonds. There is much inspiration to be found in the unsurpassed work of the whole Islamic era.

Below *A sunny corner at Charleston, where cupboards, walls, pots and all display the unmistakeable Bloomsbury hand-painted touch.*

Italy provided the next great surge of inspiration, with its Renaissance *maiolica* earthenware (named after Majorca, the point from which Spanish lustreware entered Italy). Italian potters combined classically symmetrical heraldic motifs and sacred symbols with an attempt to emulate Islamic refinement of decoration.

From Italy, potters travelled all over Europe, and many gravitated towards Delft in the Netherlands, where white tin-glazed tiles with loose, whimsical painted flora and fauna in blue, green, orange and yellow were gradually simplified and refined to the familiar and much-prized designs in blue and white.

These days, thanks to the technology of modern paints and enamels, the whole world of painted ceramics is there to plunder. A spot of complicated Italian *maiolica* should put you in the mood to tackle a relatively simple flurry of fake Mexican tiles, or to embellish a humble terracotta pot with which to grace your patio. Inspiration for designs both bold and delicate is all around.

*R*ICHARD *L*OWTHER'S *P*AINTED *C*ERAMIC *P*OTS

Left In an endless and enviable outpouring of creativity, Dick adds a flick of paint or a flurry of dots to one of his painted plant pots, taking inspiration from Greek heads, nineteenth-century bird engravings, or whatever marvels Nature produces in his garden. Behind him is a panel of fake tiles which could be copied to make a desirable bath-surround, table-top or door-panel.

Richard Lowther is a painter and sculptor, and freelance bookillustrator. He taught at Chelsea School of Art until four years ago, when he and his girlfriend, Lynne, decided that London was unbearable and moved to France. 'We can just about make a living here, with the lifeline of the telephone and the fax machine. And I was beginning to feel that I'd never grow up, because as a teacher, you're always speaking to eighteen-year-olds.'

Yet a life in northern France is no rural idyll, by any means. The majority of working hours are spent in sourcing or preparing artwork, or in travelling to London or Paris for meetings with clients. Living abroad, Lynne and Richard have to put even more effort into keeping communication channels open with clients, and the joy of fresh air, good food and beautiful scenery is firmly tempered by the freelancers' normal anxiety over money, work, no work and impossible deadlines.

Although book and magazine illustration is the mainstay of their income, they both enjoy working in other mediums. Richard has recently combined his interest in ceramics and painting by developing a range of colourful and highly original painted pots. Fascinated by the beauty and soft colours of antiquity, he sourced his Greek designs at the British Museum. 'I like the deteriorating fresco-feel of Greece and Rome. The British Museum was a natural place to find inspiration, and I was captivated by a set of stone heads of classical deities which was on display there.' He made some slides of them, projected the transparencies straight on to the gessoed pots, and then drew the outlines in pencil. 'Some people get a bit precious and they say, you're either a painter, or you're not. But Paris used to be full of artists turning their hands to other things. I'm basically the dreamy artist who'll spend all morning looking out of the window before I really get on with putting paint to paper . . . or even pot.'

PROJECT: RICHARD LOWTHER'S PAINTED CERAMIC POTS

Apollo, Juno or Athena on a classic painted pot, recalling the multi-coloured statues that scholars believe once peopled a polychrome Parthenon. To make Richard Lowther's Pompeiian pots you will need:

Materials

- Ordinary terracotta plant pots (22 cm (8¾ in) diameter in this case)
- Acrylic gesso or primer
- Tracing paper
- Masking tape
- Acrylic (Liquitex) paint: Payne's grey, yellow ochre, Venetian red, sky blue
- Matt acrylic varnish

Tools

- Large paintbrushes and artists' brushes
- Soft pencil
- Sponge
- Knife
- Wet and dry emery paper

1 Paint pot outside and inside rim with white acrylic gesso or primer. Leave to dry. Trace and enlarge the drawings shown right and on following page. Scribble over back of drawing with soft pencil, tape tracing paper to pot and transfer outlines.

2 Outline drawing with Payne's grey acrylic paint, used like watercolour. You can wipe off mistakes while wet. Detail eyes, nostrils, lips, chin and hair but don't bother with fine details such as eyelashes.

Juno

3 Apply yellow ochre all over pot as background. Before it dries, splash with water and dab off with sponge to give a faded old Pompeiian-wall look. Dab off smudgy stripes on rim in the same way. Allow to dry.

4 Scratch surface of pot lightly with knife to simulate cracks and extreme old age. Paint below rim with Venetian red (with a little brown added if you have it).

Apollo

Athena

5 Dab off colour with sponge to break texture and allow ochre to show.

6 When you are satisfied with the background of the lower part of the pot, you can then decorate the rim. Paint loose crosses in sky blue on rim with a fine brush. Allow to dry.

7 Sand very lightly all over to break up texture and reveal surface below. Sand off any rough edges.

8 Pick out and emphasize facial details with watery sky blue and sponge lines to soften. Paint inner rim. Allow to dry. Give a coat or two of matt varnish to pot inside and out to protect and waterproof it.

Left These perfectly ordinary terracotta pots have been elevated to art by a painter with a brilliant sense of colour and a skill with images. Those of us who are not painters can happily plagiarize his ideas for texture and pattern.

*L*AMPSHADES

Lampshades are the poor relations of the crafts world. Everyone needs something with which to soften the glare of their 100-watt bulbs, pearl or plain, but what to use and how to do it seems to be a creative blind spot. The problem is a relatively new one. In the past the choice was between candles, whose flickering glow does not really need shading, paraffin and oil whose flame came filtered through coloured and etched glass globes, and gas, whose green and lurid light no amount of shading could enhance.

All sorts of ingenuity goes into designing lamps and candlesticks, but none of the possibilities offered by translucent fabrics and papers, experiments with the stained-glass potential of patches of transparent acetate, or variations on the paper theme beloved of the Japanese, seem to have been exploited with lampshades. Few have tried out the soft and unevenly textured finish conferred by handmade paper; few have played with layers of coloured tissue, designed to spring to a multi-coloured life when the light is switched on; or explored the possibilities of drawing and painting – except at Charleston where the Bloomsbury group decorated just about everything – a tradition carried on today by Cressida Bell.

Lace, patterned and textured papers, beads, doilies, skeleton leaves, stencils, pinprick perforations, gold leaf: all seem to have been ignored in favour of the strange labour-intensive creations of the fifties, all bias-bound wire, pleated chiffon and blobby trimmings. The Japanese have a way with simple constructions using the most casual ingredients of bamboo and paper which cast a flattering shade. There is no reason why one should not use transparent fabrics in multi-coloured wafts if the

Above *Lampshades painted by Cressida Bell: their strong and vibrant colours glow like stained glass under the influence of electricity.*

Right *These stacks of candle and lampshades exploit a spectrum of techniques: stencils, pricked and embossed paper, découpage, painted and patterned paper, bound and scalloped edges, and touches of gilt.*

mysteries of origami are too much to explore. Indian cotton muslin comes in a huge range of colours and floats fetchingly but if all this lightness proves unmanageable, you can use a judicious bead or two to weight it into submission. Plain commercial lampshades are inexpensive and can be painted, découpaged, stencilled or punched. Pleated lampshades are available from every home interior shop but they are more exciting when they are home-made using colourful and unusual paper. In virtually every other aspect of home interiors, the discerning, design-minded consumer has learned to appreciate the charm of personality; fitted kitchens are being jettisoned in favour of a gaggle of Italian apothecary cupboards and French bakers' shelves, and the obligatory acreage of machine-made chintz ruffles of yesteryear are finding their way into the attic, to be replaced by variations on homespun with a bit of character. But lampshades still tend to look hard and shiny and new.

Above *Simple light games with lampshades – a brilliantly easy idea to copy, involving only a plain bought shade, a ruler and a craft knife.*

Once in place, people no longer seem to notice their lampshades. Every photographer and every stylist knows that lighting is the one simple thing that can make a room look inviting or utterly repellent. Lighting may be warm or cold, have many or few sources, be placed high on the ceiling or dotted low and intimate around the room, bright spots or muted pools. With this handful of variants the atmosphere can be totally altered, from glaring interrogation room to Rudolf Valentino's seduction suite. Most people look for something in between, and a change of lampshade can effect a huge improvement for very little effort.

ANDREA MAFLIN'S GILDED LAMPSHADE

Andrea Maflin's paperworks are like a diary. Her explorations in museums, researches into family archives, and abiding fascination with nature – all find expression somewhere on her lampshades, picture frames, screens, tables, trays, clocks and cupboards. She is a great advocate of the photocopier, which she uses to reproduce crisp nineteenth-century engravings, Japanese art, snatches of poetry, sketches and elegant Victorian script, to which she subsequently gives an air of antiquity with a wash of strong tea.

Having a relish for beautifully penned historic documents, much of the material she uses is taken from family deeds, and the property records of an old farm that belonged to her family: 'Everything that was bought and sold over a hundred years was meticulously written down: letters, recipes, postcards with messages, all in different handwriting. People wrote so beautifully a century ago.'

She is relentlessly inventive: she makes her living from her fabric designs – having studied textiles at art school – and her clever and elegant creations with paper and gold leaf are now sold in select shops. She has a passion for paper: 'It is so instant, and you can do so much with it: slash it and paint it, give it texture by sandpapering it or burning it; you can print on it, and then wash it and then bleach it.' For those endowed with a restless creative spirit, the possibilities are practically endless.

She is a great traveller, and values the complete detachment it allows from her work. In her constant search for new ideas, she finds inspiration everywhere, from Indonesian textiles for their graphic intricacy to Picasso and Hockney for their energy and colour. She spends hours in museums, and can be an embarrassment on country walks: 'I never go to the beach without picking up driftwood and shells and old rusty things. I've got all these bags of bits . . . I've just made a mobile out of driftwood, wire and fishbones.' She has that rare and precious attribute of being able to make you look afresh at the world and all the marvels you take for granted.

Above *Andrea painting an artichoke with a Chinese brush. Beside her is one of her large gilded and torn paper collages, and behind are her script collages of almost Oriental simplicity.*

Right *Andrea's stylish combination of flowing script and crisp engravings, sometimes gilded, sometimes antiqued using tea, casts its elegant spell over all manner of unlikely objects – tables, chests of drawers, clocks and frames, as well as lampshades.*

Below *Andrea's shell engravings for you to trace or photocopy.*

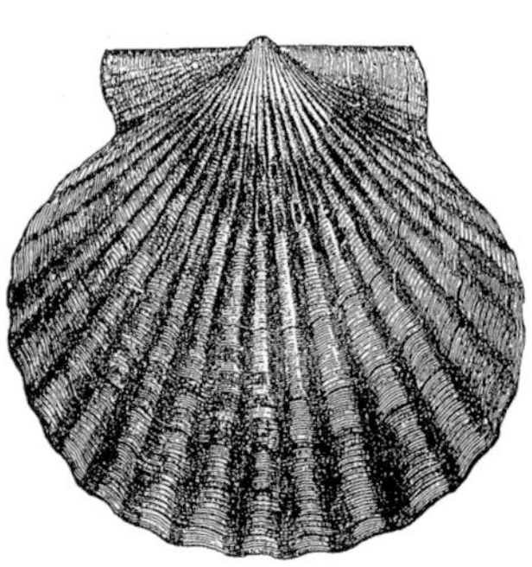

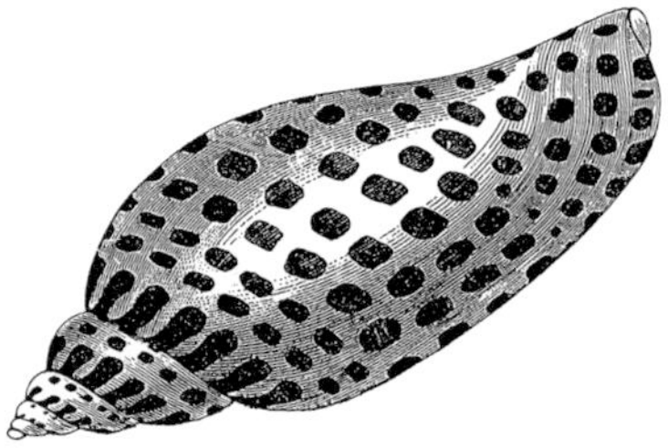

PROJECT:

*A*NDREA *M*AFLIN'S *G*ILDED *L*AMPSHADE

Given a fluent and casual touch with textured paper and gold leaf, Andrea Maflin's easy and elegant lampshade is a resourceful way to lighten your darkness.
To make Andrea's gilded lampshade you will need:

Materials

- Handmade paper
- Diluted PVA glue
- Paper or fabric-covered lampshade
- Transfer gold leaf
- Photocopies of shells or elegant writing
- Strong tea for tinting

Tools

- Paintbrush
- Jam jar
- Scissors

1 Tear handmade paper into rectangles narrower at the top than the bottom. Mix equal quantities of glue and water in a jar and paint lampshade. Starting from the top, and leaving 1.5 cm (¾ in) extra at both top and bottom, cover with overlapping paper rectangles, carefully smoothing out air bubbles as you work.

2 Trim top and bottom evenly to leave enough to cover wire frame. Using undiluted glue, stretch extra paper neatly around frame.

3 Cut transfer gold leaf roughly into quarters. Paint diluted glue on to shade where you want gold, place unbacked side of gold leaf on glue, and peel off backing. Allow to dry for one minute, then rub gently with the fingers to distress it.

4 Tint photocopied shells with strong tea. Leave to dry. Cut out carefully. Paint diluted glue on shade and smooth shells in place, removing air bubbles as before. When dry, paint the whole thing with diluted PVA glue to seal and protect it.

*P*APIER *M*ÂCHÉ

Papier mâché enjoys the universal charms of being easy to do, requiring no special tools, using cheap and freely available materials and adapting good-naturedly to whatever is demanded, whether it be to create a fearsome Chinese warrior's head-dress from the second century AD, or to confect a gilded and jewel-encrusted mask, fit for a Borgia ball. Boxes from Samarkand with delicate confetti-fine flowers painted on black, Indian candlesticks bedecked with prancing elephants on a gold ground, French lacquer chests inlaid with mother-of-pearl, utterly smooth Japanese lacquered *saké* cups, Russian folk-art trays resplendent with unseasonal bouquets, nineteenth-century German dolls, crude and joky skeletons for the Mexican Day of the Dead, Italian puppets, Victorian letter-racks and pen trays, wings for the Angel Gabriel at the school Christmas play – every era and culture worth its salt has toyed with papier mâché, and exploited its lightness, strength and affinity to paint. In seventeenth-century Norway, an entire church was constructed out of papier mâché, and the congregation worshipped in this paper temple for thirty-seven years until it was finally demolished.

Above *A Matisse-bright lacquered papier mâché bowl, making a surprisingly sympathetic home for a handful of wooden grooming aids of Oriental air.*

Right *Small winged bowls by Juliette Pearce in a nest of shredded paper – if you yearn for a six-handled bowl, you can have one; papier mâché is endlessly amenable.*

Far right *Utterly smooth texture, wonderfully broken paint – an Arabic-flavoured bowl by Madeleine Adams.*

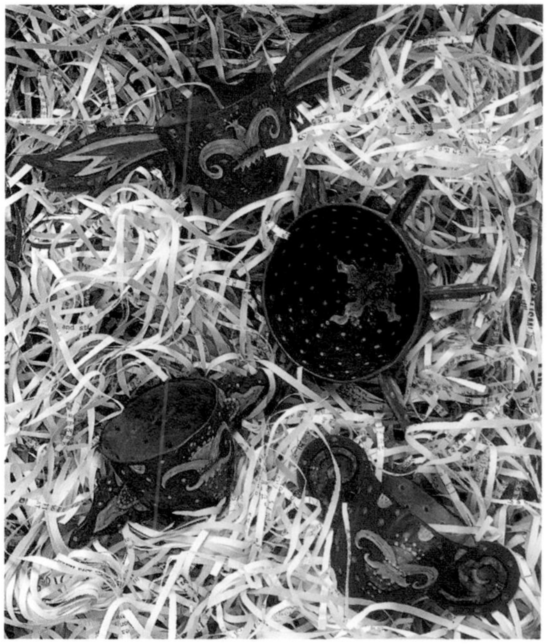

It is simplicity itself to reproduce the shape of an existing bowl, dish or tray of

Right *Any right-minded hen's idea of a handsome rooster, constructed by Margaret Frere-Smith to strut proudly in his bold papier mâché livery.*

glass, ceramic or metal. Shells, stones, fossilized ammonites, jelly moulds, cookie cutters – there are all sorts of things to plunder for moulds. And because the materials cost virtually nothing, papier mâché is a liberating invitation to experiment and indulge in fond pastiche. You can make your mould with Plasticine if no existing shape comes to hand – particularly with masks and jewellery, where you are unlikely to find the perfect model. There are two basic consistencies of soaked paper – the smooth finish conferred by carefully layered torn strips, and the rougher somewhat porridgy texture from using pulped paper. Again, experimentation is your best guide, whether you want sophistication or a dash of ethnic *élan*.

Armed with a pile of soaked paper, some paste, an hour or two, and a mad missionary light in your eyes, you can cunningly copy and improve on prohibitively expensive Christmas tree decorations, and speedily turn out a whole production line of gilded stars; you can try découpage or stencils; you can lay a veil of transparent tissue

Left Educational fun in the classroom. A magnificent donkey, convincing in every way despite his (as yet) naked cardboard and wire mesh armature.

Above *The future Green Party sporting carrot, turnip and radish masks ready for an impromptu greengrocers' masked ball.*

over the newsprint, incorporate ornate buttons, cut-glass beads, pieces of broken china, string, skeleton leaves, silver and gold foil or just about anything that amuses you – in inflationary times you may care to deck your dishes with torn bank-notes. Different papers behave in different ways, some are more absorbent and flexible than others, and this is another feature to exploit. You may enjoy the ragged edges of your creation, or cut the rim with perfectionist precision, finishing by punctilious bevelling and sanding.

Wallpaper paste has thankfully been superseded by quick-drying glues such as Marvin medium, which can also act as a vehicle for paint and a sealer for the finished object. No longer do you have to transform your airing cupboard into a mould incubator while your art object refuses to dry out in readiness for the next layer of torn paper. These days the whole business can be completed straight away – and you can be much more adventurous with finishes and special effects. You might like to try marbling, dipping your creation cautiously in commercial ceramic or glass paint suspended in a bowl of water. When dry and sealed, papier mâché is surprisingly strong and has many of the virtues of ceramics – the mouldable plastic quality and affinity to colour – with none of the faults. You do not need a kiln, you do not have to be privy to the arcana of glazes and temperatures, the whole thing will not mysteriously distort in its construction, nor will it break if it falls from your over-excited fingers. And should you wish to, you can make turnip masks and pantomime horses which are light enough to prance about the chorus in.

*M*ARION *E*LLIOT'S *P*APIER-MÂCHÉ *M*ONEY-BOX

Folk art, medieval art, popular art, packaging, advertising art, circus and fairground painting, Staffordshire figurines, churches and religious ephemera, and kitsch – just about anything bright and bold is a source of inspiration to Marion Elliot.

She started off by studying fine art, and went on to do a post-graduate course in ceramics. She has no time for porridgy hand-thrown clay, being drawn much more to tin-glazed maiolica, with which she struggled, before falling foul of its unpredictability: 'I got fed up with the technical irritations of glazes. I like Mexican things made out of clay, and painted with house-paints. I had loads of plaster moulds, and I decided to use them for papier mâché instead, and paint with gouache.'

This she did, with great relief 'I taught myself how to use papier mâché – it's so easy after messing around with clay. I was leaving college and just did not have the money to set up a kiln. It was a perfect DIY way of making things', although not without its pitfalls. Her first experiments were with that disastrous old-fashioned expedient – wallpaper paste – and she ended up with a house full of rotting paper. 'I tried making pulp – it was messy and awful. I like a smooth surface, that's why I use paper strips. I try to make it very smooth. It took three or four months to get it right, and I just carried on from there.'

The quality of newspaper is also all important, and Marion frankly admits that her choice of daily broadsheet is now based solely on the thickness of its paper. Using a cardboard armature or a Plasticine mould means that she can make bigger and more challenging things than the usual candlesticks and bowls. A 6ft 6in mirror resplendent with cherubs, sun and moon for a New York men's shop for instance, or a puppet theatre. For the kitchen-table craft enthusiast, papier mâché has all the advantages of ceramics, plus simplicity and fun. And perhaps best of all, the ingredients cost nothing and enable you to catch up with the news.

Left Subtlety is not Marion's middle name, but she has an irrepressible streak of irreverence and fun that gets to the heart of what crafts are all about. To become utterly absorbed in drawing an elephant, or in the interplay of this red with that blue, is to return to the enchanted world of childhood, where time is forgotten and gas bills are irrelevant.

Above Piratical boxes in which to stash your treasures, alive with vigorous drawing and unabashed colour.

PROJECT: *MARION ELLIOT'S PAPIER-MÂCHÉ MONEY-BOX*

A diminutive and eclectic country cottage, in which to save your spare change.
To make Marion Elliot's cottage money-box you will need:

Materials

- Heavy card
- Masking tape
- Diluted PVA glue
- Newspaper
- White emulsion paint
- Poster and gouache paints
- Waterproof black ink
- Clear gloss varnish

Tools

- Pencil
- Craft knife
- Steel rule
- Cutting mat
- Scissors
- Paint and varnish brushes

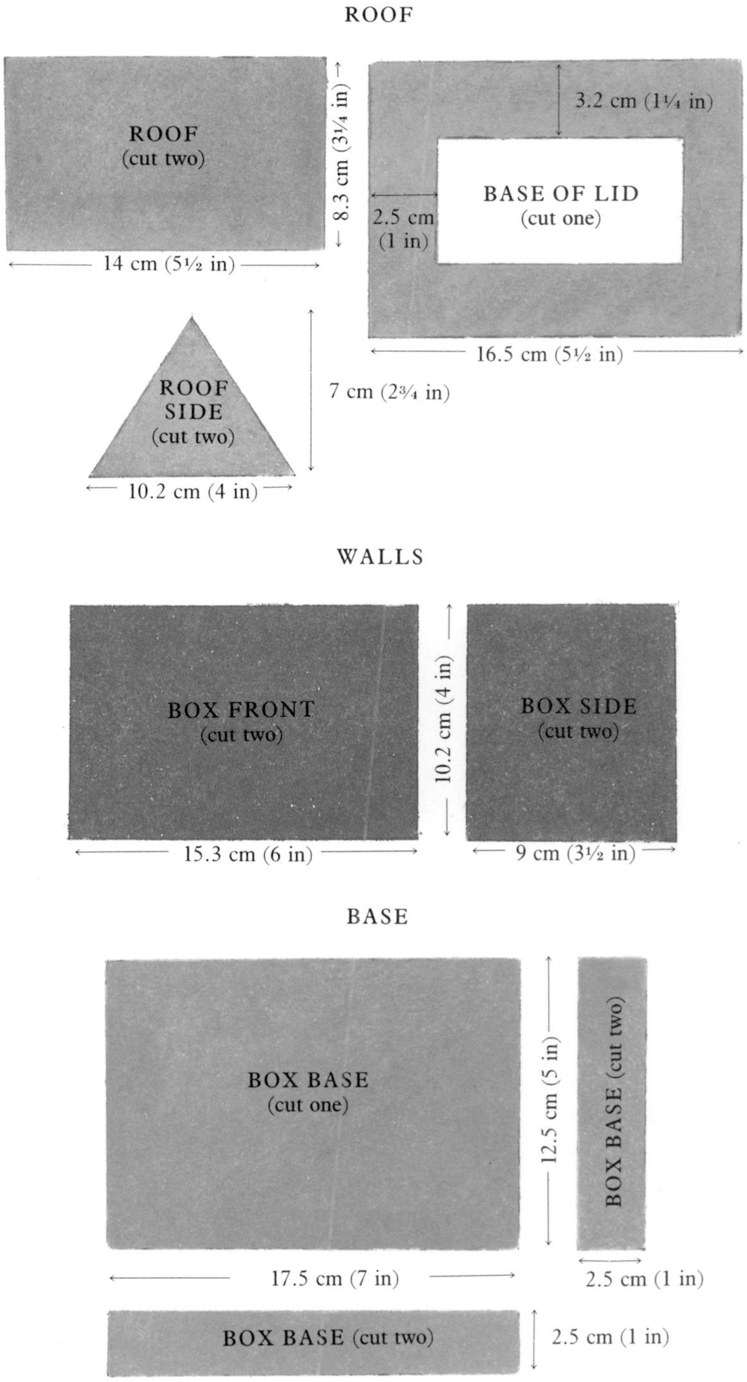

1 Draw house components on to heavy card. Cut out carefully. Cut neat slit in one roof side for money. Cut out middle of roof base board to allow money to fall into house. Glue and tape basic structure together as shown and position and tape roofline.

2 Cover the entire box both inside and out with four or five layers of newspaper strips glued in place with diluted PVA glue. Allow to dry.

3 Prime with white emulsion and draw design freehand on front, back, sides, base and roof. Make the elements big and bold, and have fun with the faces at the windows.

4 Paint the base, background and details. For roof texture use successively darker tones of paint with a dry brush. Thicken up the black lines with waterproof black ink. Place roof on house. Seal with 2 coats of clear varnish.

*F*LOTSAM AND *J*ETSAM

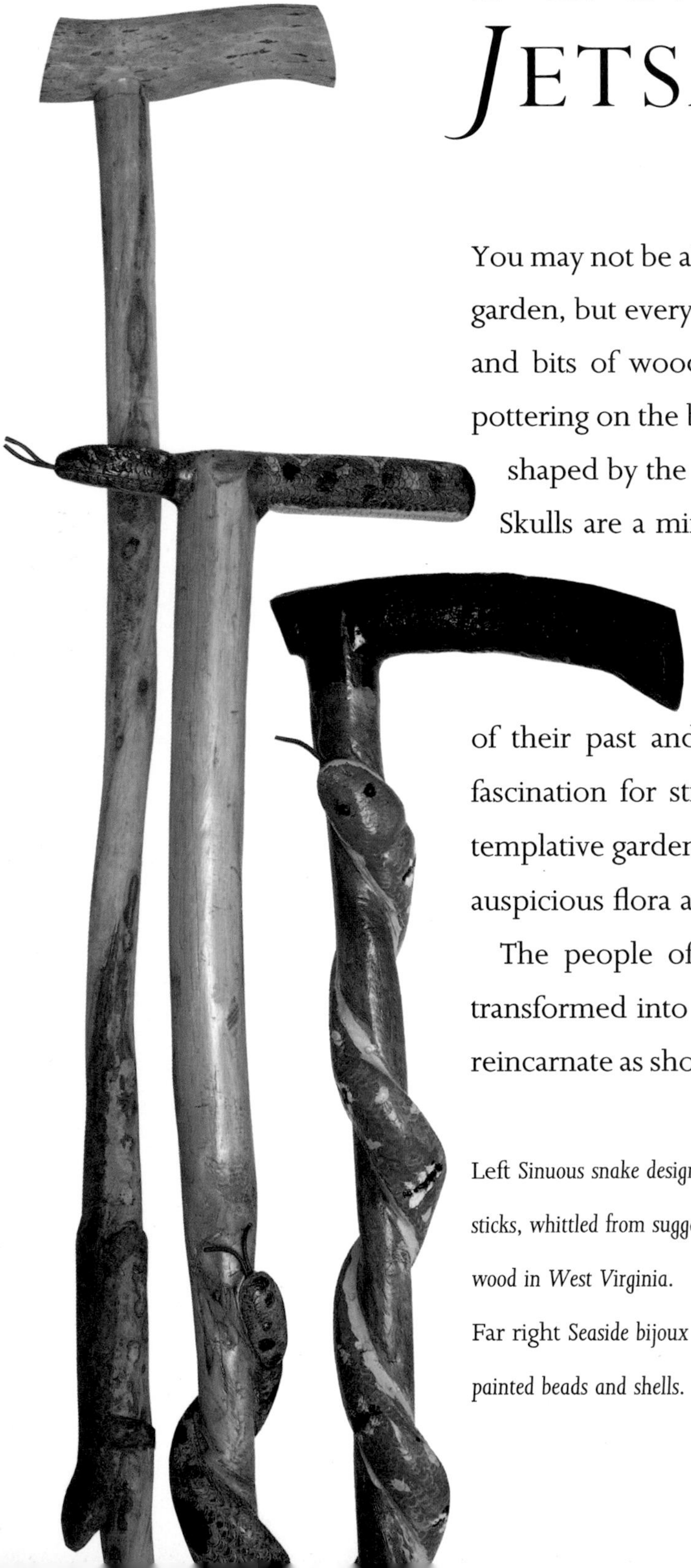

You may not be able to afford a massive reclining nude by Henry Moore for your back garden, but everyone can find inspiration where he did in interesting stones, feathers and bits of wood. Most artists worth their salt have, while striding the moors or pottering on the beach, discovered and collected natural objects – gnarled, bitten and shaped by the whims of weather and water – from which they have derived ideas. Skulls are a minority interest shared by the Prince of Denmark and the American artist Georgia O'Keefe, but sea-sculpted spars, ghostly ammonites petrified in rock, shells of every kind, feathers, and perfectly shaped pebbles, have a universal appeal arising perhaps from the mysteries of their past and provenance. The Chinese and the Japanese have always had a fascination for stream-polished rocks which hold a place of honour in their contemplative gardens, where paths of smooth, dark and light pebbles laid in a mosaic of auspicious flora and fauna wind through bamboo groves.

The people of India are magpies *par excellence* – anything shiny is likely to be transformed into some article of clothing, and metallic chewing gum wrappers may reincarnate as shopping bags with armadillo scales of silver. Clothes are encrusted with Shisha embroidery characterized by specks of mirror glass, and cowrie shells. In a tradition of ephemeral and auto-destructive art, propitious patterns are traced on the ground in flower petals, and a stranger will be greeted with a floral garland to sweeten the air he breathes for an hour or two.

Left *Sinuous snake design walking sticks, whittled from suggestive twisted wood in West Virginia.*

Far right *Seaside bijoux of raffia, painted beads and shells.*

Left Spot the crafts among the spars: a high-water mark of witty boats, frames and mirrors conjured up from the results of beady-eyed beach-combing, summon recollections of blustery days at the seaside, and the mysterious detritus of the ocean.

The people of Africa also maintain a grand tradition for creative recycling, making brilliant Imbenge bowls from discarded telephone cable, and surreal skeletons of cars, boats and bicycles from snipped fencing wire and bottle tops. Egg cartons turn into frilly shelf edgings; car hub-caps prolong their lives as highly polished wall features.

North-American Indians were the champions of economy, and displayed ingenuity with whatever materials came to hand. The Pomo had a strong talent for decoration, and their ceremonial baskets were elegantly tufted with quail and woodpecker feathers. Every bit of a dead animal was put to some use by the North-American Indians. The dreaded drum-beats harkened to in many a cinema Western, emanated from animal skin stretched over a hollow log, perhaps accompanied by a wash-board rhythm section rattling a stick along a deer shoulder blade or shaking some stones in a gourd. Deer anklebones came in useful as *ad hoc* dice, as did beaver teeth. Antlers became spoons, bracelets, harpoons and combs.

Above *A mussel-bound shelf and mirror in homage to the beauty of bivalves and the glory of gastropods. In a rustic interior, what better way to recall picnics in pine forests and walks along the shore at sunset?*

More familiarly the Victorians, who had a passion for productive fidgeting, were the masters of *objets trouvés*, and used them to improve their leisure hours. They created seed, sand and feather pictures; composed shell bouquets; made trays bearing brilliant landscapes entirely concocted of beetles' and butterflies' wings; and constructed the Taj Mahal from matchsticks. One has to sympathize with the legion of nimble-fingered ladies doomed to a lifetime's excess of such Sisyphean leisure.

Fortunately, most people are now in a position to exercise some choice over their liberty. If pinprick pictures are your passion, you can steam ahead, but if bucolic sophistication appeals, then you can commemorate a flawless summer's day of beach-combing with a more speedily made and handsome souvenir.

JOAN MOLLOY'S FLOTSAM CLOCK

Somehow one expects clocks to be the province of the ancient and weathered. Joan Molloy, who looks all of sixteen, comes as something of a surprise among this hoary fraternity. Her passion at Art School was for sculpture, mixed with a Celtic penchant for poetry. She is fascinated by remnants of things, clues and memories: 'The things that you need to survive, the things you take with you and the remnants you leave behind', and she used to haunt the Egyptian department of the British Museum entranced by the poignant luggage deemed necessary for the afterlife.

Clocks began with a Christmas present for her mother: 'My father made the box, I got hold of a really nice old litho plate and I found this illustration of Descartes explaining how the eye works – all to do with lenses – and I put a dial on the round shape of the eye.' Soon, Liberty's and The Designer's Guild asked her to make some for their shops in London, and she found that they were disappearing fast to Japan, Canada, America and Switzerland. Recently, the Bodleian Library in Oxford asked her to make a clock to celebrate its manuscript collection.

Her largest clock is a tryptich made in homage to William Blake. It incorporates snatches of his poetry written on wood, and the themes of earth, fire and water are expressed by the motley objects framed in each section: slate, earth and corn; burnt straw, guttered candle stubs, a flame-coloured scarlet background; and a final cool blue frame awash with shells and oceanic references.

She likes natural and weathered objects best, mixed with a symbolic collection of maps, compasses, scraps of correspondence, keys, old photographs and lights – a sort of frozen moment of meaningful fragments with clues to the past and portents of the future. For her own pleasure, she dispenses with the clockface, and just enjoys the objects. 'The ones that I really like, I give to friends, so that I can go and see them. I gave one to my sister when my nephew Conor was born, with the date of his birth and his weight painted on, and one to my brother when he got married.' She has such a poetic way with the significant paraphernalia of life, that she has been inundated with various bits and pieces and asked to make artworks of them – the greatest challenge being a honeymoon souvenir decorated with Japanese karaoke lyrics.

Above *Joan Molloy at work with a magpie collection of feathers, leaves, pebbles, ferns, wheatstalks and shells, a collection with a country common denominator that would look good even without her inspired and poetic framing.*

Overleaf *Timepieces: a collection of clocks to die for. Joan Molloy's haunting documentations of passing time combine souvenirs of places visited, events recorded, good intentions and wisps of music, with echoes of Magritte. Such poetry leaves quartz clocks standing.*

JAPAN

POST CARD

PROJECT:

JOAN MOLLOY'S FLOTSAM CLOCK

A timepiece with memories – Joan Molloy's clock recalls days by the seashore, beach-huts and seagulls. *Tempus fugit* in a nostalgic frame.

To make Joan's evocative clock you need:

Materials

- 2 lengths of pine for box-frame 43 cm (17 in) long, 1 cm (½ in) thick
- 2 lengths of pine for box-frame 24 cm (9½ in) long, 1 cm (½ in) thick
- At least 137 cm (54 in) picture framing pine for front, 5 mm (²⁄₁₀ in) thick
- At least 125 cm (49 in) wooden beading 2.5×1 cm (1×½ in)
- 2 mm (¹⁄₁₆ in) thick glass, cut to fit frame
- Plastic wood
- Tongued and grooved pine strips, 5×35 mm (¼×1½ in)
- Jade-green non-drip gloss paint
- Araldite glue
- Battery-operated quartz clock mechanism
- Batteries
- Feathers, shells or pebbles
- Clock dial
- Glass beading
- 2 cm (¾ in) and 1 cm (½ in) panel pins

Tools

- Saw
- G-clamps
- Hammer
- Medium grade sandpaper
- Paintbrushes
- Nail punch

1 Cut ends of wood for box-frame at 45 degree angles to make mitred corners. Glue, G-clamp and nail into position.

2 Cut strips of beading to fit tightly inside frame. Nudge it down 2 mm (1/16 in) so that glass can fit flush with the top, and nail in place with 2 cm (3/4 in) panel pins.

3 Measure inside of box frame, and buy glass slightly smaller to fit, leaving some play. Cut picture framing pine to fit over glass on box frame and mitre the corners. Pin and glue with glass in place.

4 Punch 2 cm (3/4 in) panel pins home, and fill with plastic wood. Sand whole box thoroughly. Paint with a thin layer of non-drip gloss paint on bare wood. Allow to dry. Sand gently with medium sandpaper to bring out the grain of the wood.

5 Cut lengths of tongued and grooved pine to fit back of box. Paint and sand as before. Stick pebbles, feathers or shells in place with Araldite. Drill 1 cm (1/2 in) hole where you want centre of dial. Screw mechanism to back of clock-face. Attach dial and hands. Position clock-face in frame and secure in place with glass beading and 1 cm (1/2 in) panel pins. Attach with wall brackets or picture hooks to wall.

BOOKBINDING

The Egyptians liked to travel light, and although books in the form of clay bricks could serve several functions, convenience was not one of them and so they began to use a form of paper made from water reeds known as papyrus. With the introduction of vellum parchment around the first century BC, books could be made in the familiar and more usable codex form, derived from the Latin word *caudex* meaning tree-trunk, because in Rome it was customary to use sheets of wood for the book-boards. Unlike papyrus, parchment sheets could be quite big. They were flexible and hardwearing, and they could take writing on both sides.

Above *Fine block-printed oriental papers, textured with interesting imperfections, and requiring no great artistry to be transformed into notebooks or folders.*

Far right *A work-table busy with the fascinating accoutrements of the grand age of letter-writing – candle, wax and signet, and a stack of thick, satisfying paper and envelopes spattered with bright seals.*

During the Middle Ages, the existing libraries of books in Europe were protected in monasteries where scribes plied their quills for as long as daylight lasted, copying the texts in special rooms or scriptoria. When these sacred texts had been committed to vellum, the monks sought to increase the glory of their handiwork by binding the pages in miracles of the jeweller's, embroiderer's, goldsmith's or ivory carver's skill. These advances were not restricted exclusively to Europe, however. In Egypt, the Coptic Church produced red and brown goatskin covers which were rich in craftsmanship. The legendary Koran bindings of red Morocco leather were already veiled with a refined filigree of gold embossing by the fourteenth century, and from Persia at this time came delicate floral designs, bright doublures (inside flaps), and protective coats of lacquer.

France and Italy were the bookbinders *par excellence* in Europe from the sixteenth century, taking much of their inspiration from oriental and Islamic embroidery and metalwork pattern books. An English addition to the bookbinder's range of decorative

finishes was the technique of fore-edge painting, in which the usual gilt edge of the closed book could be splayed out to reveal a painting of flowers or scenery.

Fine bookbinding is a delicate art, and the final product involves a great many specialist skills. The use of leather complicates the procedure because it has to be shaved to an even thickness, a procedure known as skiving, which is fraught with expensive mistakes for the novice. For economic reasons full leather bindings are a rarity except for precious books, and the half and quarter bindings were designed to make the best use of the strength and flexibility of small pieces of leather by combining them with paper or cloth. Books with cloth or leather spines and corners are known as half-bound in Britain but three-quarter bound in the United States; books without corners are generally described as quarter-bound in Britain – and half- or French-bound in the United States.

Below *Decorative marbled papers to transform any book into a work of art.*

Right *A de luxe scrap-book for your most treasured souvenirs.*

The tooling of the title on the spine and decoration on the front is a further art requiring vision, precision and a steady hand. One mistake, and the bookbinder has to scrap the whole thing and start again. Fortunately bookbinding does not always have to aspire to such heights, and handsome folders and notebooks. Today, some contemporary bookbinders have already blazed a trail for us, making a virtue of less precise bindings. Some of the most presentable covers are simple flaps of soft, jewel-coloured leather; others make a virtue out of their intensely humble origins, using a swathe of utility fabric to conceal the crunchy wad of recycled paper within.

*R*OB *S*HEPHERD'S *S*HELL-PATTERNED *P*ORTFOLIO

Rob Shepherd took up bookbinding after graduating from a fine-art course in painting. During a short spell of teaching, he learnt how to make books at an evening class and his interest in the craft has continued to grow ever since.

He began with absolutely no equipment: 'I got used to the notion of doing everything with very basic tools – I used to weight drying work with a sheet of plywood and old irons', a method he still uses, though now, since he restores rare and precious books, he has a wide range of specialist bookbinding tools at his disposal.

He has always loved beautiful bindings, and even as a boy, would spend many happy hours in second-hand bookshops. 'I took up bookbinding in the beginning just to rebind my own books. My tastes have become simpler as I've got older – and I can now appreciate various aspects of the trade which I didn't value before, such as the ancient bookbinding traditions of Japan or the expertise of the nineteenth-century trade binders.'

His work is characterized by its unpretentious good looks. He does not classify bookbinding as 'art', preferring to regard his work as a continuation of a traditional craft. He draws inspiration from the traditions of Europe – silk-screen printing his own version of eighteenth-century Italian woodblock papers for instance – as well as from the work of modern fabric designers such as Bentley and Spens who contributed the design for the project.

To make Rob's portfolio, you can plunder the beautiful and irresistible papers that you could never quite think what to do with before. Your portfolio will magically endow your hoarded bits and pieces with charm and significance; as every collector knows, the most important documents become trashed when they accrete in an old shoe-box, but frame a tattered tram-ticket and it will suddenly become a work of art.

Above left *Rob Shepherd at work in his studio surrounded by the tools of his trade.*

Above right *A treasure trove of beautiful colours and patterns.*

PROJECT: *ROB SHEPHERD'S SHELL-PATTERNED PORTFOLIO*

A handsome portfolio to dignify the nostalgic paraphernalia of life, whether theatre programmes, postcards, love letters or a collection of drawings.

To make Rob Shepherd's 30×42 cm (12×16¾ in) portfolio you will need:

Materials

- Decorative patterned fabric at least 50×50 cm (20×20 in) or larger, depending on the size of the pattern.
- Thin bank paper to line and glue-proof fabric at least 50×50 cm (20×20 in)
- Ready-filled bookcloth (contact Rob Shepherd, see page 189) for corners and spine
- Linen tape 7 mm×52 cm (¼×20¼ in) cut in half
- At least 60×84 cm (24×34 in) of 2 mm (⅛ in) thick greyboard or pulp board for front and back pieces. Not too thick or too hard to cut
- At least 45×45 cm (18×18 in) finer card for flaps
- Lining paper (dove grey Ingres paper)
- Sugar paper for interlining
- PVA glue
- Tracing paper

Tools

- Stanley knife
- Cutting mat
- Steel rule
- Glue brush
- Bone folder or smooth-edged strip of wood
- Weights and board to flatten
- Chisel

Board measurements as shown here:

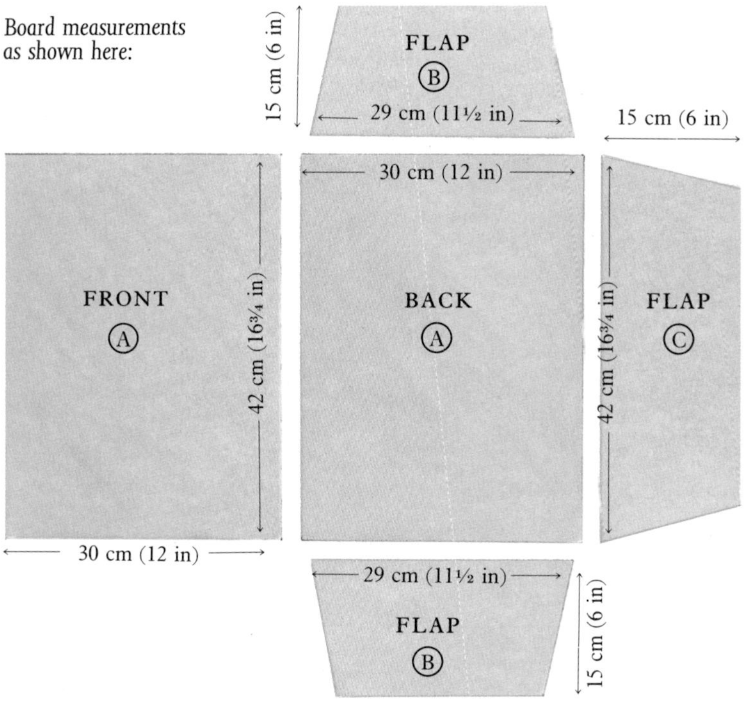

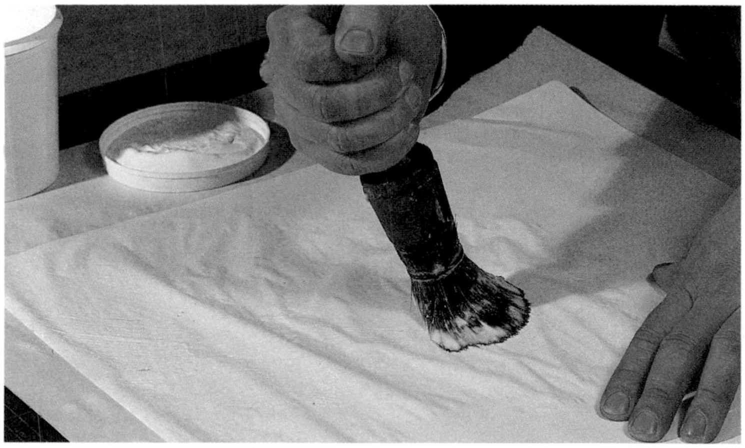

1 Back fabric with bank paper. Spread bank paper with a thick coat of PVA glue and allow to dry slightly until tacky. Position and drop fabric on to paper.

2 Smooth out air bubbles from the centre outwards, using a strip of smooth wood, or a bone folder. Flatten beneath a weight to dry.

3 Make a cardboard template of a triangle with the top cut off, and use to cut the 4 front and back corner pieces from bookcloth, to a size that looks right. The finished corner triangles are 8.5×8.5×12 cm (3¼×3¼×4¾ in). Allow 2 cm (1 in) turnings on the shorter sides and 50 mm (¼ in) overlap on the longer side. Cut out 4 pieces for the spine, 2 each of 29×1 cm (11½×½ in) and 42×2 cm (16¾×¾ in).

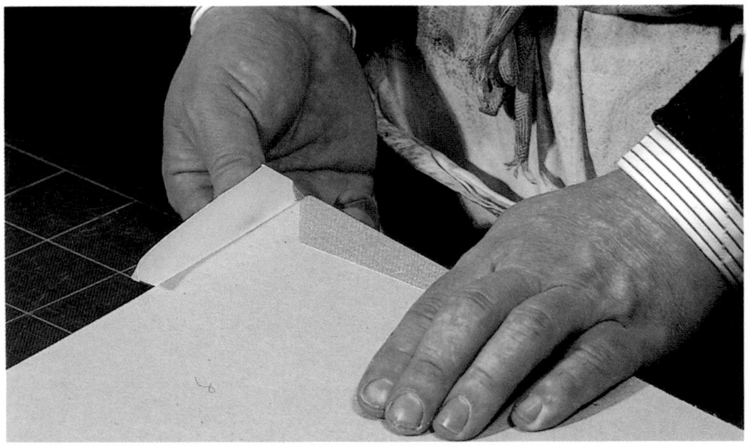

4 Using PVA glue, carefully stick corners and spine in place. Trim turnings if necessary.

5 Cut template for patterned fabric with tracing paper, allowing a 5 mm (¼ in) overlap with spine and corners, and a 1 cm (½ in) turning on front and sides. With a large fabric design, manoeuvre the template carefully to get the best pattern for front and back, mark and cut.

6 Glue paper backing and attach to front and back boards, smoothing out towards the corners. Overlap spine and corners by 5 mm (¼ in). Trim if necessary.

7 Cut spine lining from bookcloth 40×4 cm (16×1½ in) and glue in place, curving and pressing into position. Shape inside of spine with bone smoother.

8 Glue outer side of each flap with plain backed fabric allowing extra 4.5 cm (1¾ in) on longest edge of each piece. Dry flat. Make a hole on fabric side in the middle of the shorter sides of the smaller flaps for tapes, ½ cm (¼ in) from edge. Thread tapes through and tap tape and hole flat. Secure 1.5 cm (¾ in) tape with PVA at back. Trim fabric and lining paper flush with the card except on long edges.

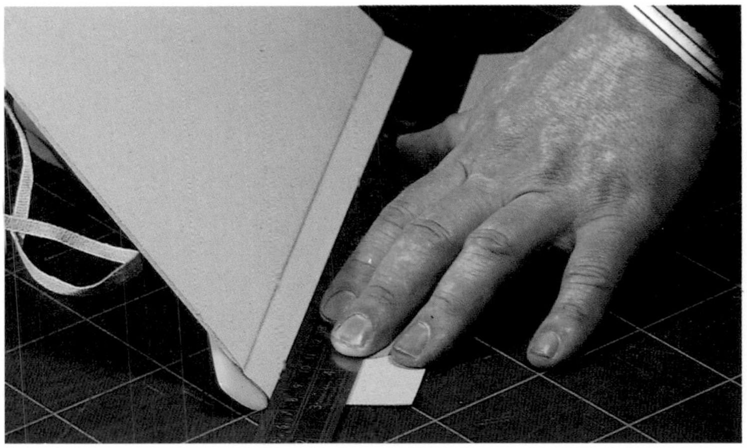

9 Using a steel rule, bend the flaps on the lining side along the edge of the card and 3 cm (1¼ in) from the edge, where the flaps will attach to the inside of portfolio front. Glue in place flush with portfolio edges. Dry under a weight.

10 At this stage, perfectionists line the card inside with sugar paper, cutting it to fit within turnings to even out the finished surface. Glue card, not sugar paper, and attach. Line the inside front and back with lining paper and trim to fit.

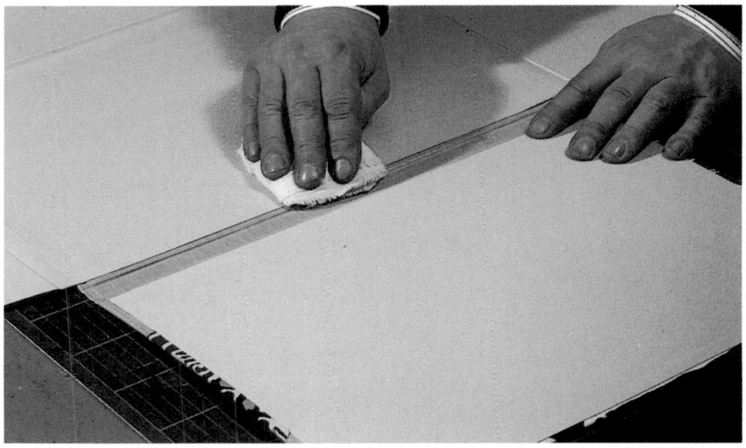

11 Press lining firmly in place. Dry under weights for at least 24 hours.

*P*AINTED *F*URNITURE

The Scandinavians are the undisputed masters of painted country furniture. Surrounded by ubiquitous pine-forests, they have understandably capitalized on this natural asset, and filled their houses with simple functional wooden furniture painting it in most subtle combinations of matt, almost transparent, colour, through which the warmth of the yellowing timber still glows. The characteristic translucency comes from the technique by which colour is built up in layers on the bare wood, with no undercoat to mask grain and texture. The unselfconscious Nordic fluency with wood comes from centuries of intimacy – ancient Norse mythology centres on a gigantic tree, Yggdrasil, whose roots tap the underworld and whose topmost twigs touch the stars.

Until recently, most wooden furniture in Norway and Sweden was painted in colours hand-mixed with linseed oil from freely-available earth pigments. This primitive technology had one glorious advantage over modern techniques and materials – it is almost impossible to make earth pigments disagree with one another. Any two make a happy marriage, add more and the mixture becomes a rich harmony, rarely ending in argument. The raw materials included rich yellow ochre, ambiguous warm greenish browns

Above *A painted floral chest from France, painted in just four main colours, is worth copying for its calm and battered dignity.*

Right *Details of clever contemporary pastiches – no more antique than tomorrow's newspaper.*

Far right *Charleston Farm with its characteristic air of creative chaos, which still inspires devoted plagiarism.*

Right *A stack of handsome boxes, painted with scenes of everyday life and architecture in eighteenth- and nineteenth-century New England. A burnt umber glaze is an essential requisite for anyone wishing to emulate this air of antiquity.*

such as raw sienna and Vandyke brown, glowing red-browns – *caput mortuum*, English red and burnt sienna – and the calming and familiar blues and greens mixed from cobalt and terre-verte. Traditionally, the Swedes had a talent with colour and paint, and they experimented boldly with spattering (*stenkmålning*), an exuberant, unconvincing fake known as farmer marbling, stencilling (*schablonmålning*), pictorial (*kurbits*) painting and the decorative hand-wrought floral patterns called *rosmålning*. Transparent tinted overglazes further harmonized the finish and lent a flattering antiquity.

Below *A fiercely feline throne, carved and painted with wit, and a perennial source of pleasure for all who sit thereon. The faintly Moorish, painted door, betrays an irreverent sense of fun and experimentation.*

In the nineteenth century, the laurels passed from Scandinavia, via Germany and Switzerland, to the Pennsylvania Dutch whose daughters dignified their marriages with gloriously decorated dower chests crammed with a lifetime's fine stitching. Integrated in the design would be the bride's name and the date when she acquired the chest. Each county was expert in its own traditional motifs: here are to be found painted unicorns (guardians of maidenhood) in Berks County, and tulips in Lebanon County. In Lancaster County they favoured architectural features, and the painters of Montgomery and Lehigh used geometric designs. The preferred combinations of red and yellow were the colours of Donar, the god of marriage and domesticity. The dower chests, and the much rarer cupboards, wardrobes, chests of drawers and grandfather clocks bear a very close similarity to their European antecedents.

The painters of America brought a lively exuberance to the traditions of the European countries from which they had originated. Given the limited palette of home-

made earth pigments, they managed to fill their homes with colour, and everything that could be, was painted. They drew on much the same repertoire of paint techniques, and completed their handiwork with an antiquing finish of raw umber in varnish or turpentine, rubbed down with powdered pumice and crude oil.

In Great Britain, softwood country furniture was painted for protection usually in the plain soft casein colours, based on a protein found in milk, that are associated with the Shakers – greens, grey-blues, foxy reds and browns – most of which was unfortunately taken back to bare wood in the time of the great stripped-pine fetish. The British have always been fond of brown interiors with a preponderance of plain or carved polished wood. There was in any case no vernacular tradition for ornate painted furniture until Duncan Grant and Vanessa Bell, the creative energy behind Bloomsbury, ran amok in their home at Charleston, and Roger Fry founded the Omega workshop where he produced 'plain, ill-constructed furniture covered with vivid, painted patterns. The designers of this furniture were wholly preoccupied with colour and indifferent to, and apparently ignorant of, structural common sense.' This supercilious dismissal (in John Gloag's *A Short Dictionary of Furniture*) ignores the lasting impact that the bright, iconoclastic effusions of this group made on a world to whom the safe, the familiar, the brown and grey, had become something of a prison.

Above *A somewhat surreal still-life with basin, anemones, twigs and delicately painted chair. The small motifs, worn away by time, have a disproportionate impact on a very humble piece of furniture.*

Right *An example of the virtues of plainness – battered and scratched casein paint of the most amenable and indeterminate bluish grey-green makes a flattering contrast for almost anything, and bestows this two-dimensional terrier with something approaching dignity.*

At Charleston everything was painted. Dogs and cats had to skitter speedily through the kitchen lest they emerge covered in cupids. Inspiration came from ancient Greece, Africa, Nature, Matisse, and Mondrian, along with a brimming cornucopia of eclectic influences. The Bloomsbury group taught a valuable lesson about the enjoyment of theatrical effects, whilst proving that the sky does not fall in if you break the rules. If painted furniture, however ill-constructed, brings pleasure, paint and be damned.

Below Cressida's sketch for her shelves is characteristically bold and confident. While such casual mastery of line and colour may elude some of us, the exercise is a useful one. Those who approach such things with trepidation, may prefer to photocopy the black-and-white outline in order to try out different patterns and colours.
Right *A dazzling handful of Cressida's productions. Like many of the most creative craftspeople, she does not live in awe of rules and has a passion for experimentation.*
Far right *At work in her East London studio, Cressida Bell lives in a kaleidoscopic world. Taking ideas from anything that crosses her path – from playing-cards to Persian miniatures – she infuses them with her own brilliant alchemy of colour.*

CRESSIDA BELL'S FRUITY SHELVES

In her studio in East London, Cressida Bell works at what she terms her cottage industry, producing screen-printed scarves, rugs and carpets, painted terracotta and furniture without the assistance of outworkers. 'I do my own screen-printing. My attitude to painted furniture is the same: it's like printing because you get quick results. I don't like things to take too long.' For this reason, she does not spend a lot of time on such niceties as preparatory sanding down, or primer: 'Your piece of furniture should be fairly cheap so that if it falls apart you go off and paint another one.' Painting things is a family habit, whether walls, tables, cupboards or doors. Cressida also paints loudspeakers, roller blinds, lampshades and pots.

For inspiration she travels whenever finances allow: to Turkey for textiles, Spain for pottery, or Sicily for general stimulation. She recommends the familiar trick of thinking about the negative, rather than the positive shapes: 'Think about the interstices of your design – you often end up with something better that way.' At home in London, she gets ideas from African textiles, silks and cottons from 'little India' in Southall, and jazzy Caribbean cotton prints covered in big hearts or footballs and championship cups: 'They have a very enlivening effect on small children.'

PROJECT: *CRESSIDA BELL'S FRUITY SHELVES*

A small set of shelves, painted in spice and fruit colours with a dash of panache and in fond recollection of the Omega Workshops.

To make Cressida's fruity shelves you will need:

Materials

- A piece of furniture: cheap and cheerful junk, the transformation is the whole point. Wash if necessary, or clean with meths or white spirit. If it is pre-varnished, sand down to provide a key for paint.
- Undercoat – vinyl matt emulsion
- A selection of water-based paints
- Water-based pigment or gouache to colour paint (not watercolour ink which fades)
- Varnish, matt or clear polyurethane
- White spirit to clean brushes

Tools

- 6 cm (2½ in) woodwork paintbrush
- Medium artist's brush
- Fine artist's brush
- Sketchbook
- Pencil
- Rubber
- Ruler
- Set square
- Cloth for mopping and dabbing
- Pots for mixing colours such as film canisters and jam jars with lids

Left *Customized shelves with an imaginative hand-painted motif. With confidence you can draw your design straight on to the painted surface, using a ruler for the straight lines on the edges, and glasses or tins as templates for the circles.*

1 Paint your piece of furniture with 2 coats of pale yellow emulsion paint. Allow to dry. Transfer your chosen design onto the painted surface, either freehand or using a stencil.

2 Mix enough paint to complete the job all in one go. Try not to cover dark with light paint, and avoid a heavy build-up of paint. With an artist's brush, paint the yellow ochre background to all the leaves, making sure you do not overlap your pencilled design lines where the pale background yellow will show through. Allow to dry.

3 Paint oranges, allow to dry, and then paint the black lines around all the edges with a fine brush, watering down the black to get a good flow of paint.

4 Paint the little white highlights on all the leaves with a free-and-easy technique, before adding blobs for the berries. Allow to dry then apply matt varnish.

DIRECTORY OF CRAFTSPEOPLE

The following is a list of the contemporary craftspeople who are actively producing craftwork in the UK and US. Page numbers indicate where work appears in the book.

NEEDLECRAFT

AMISH AND MENNONITE QUILTS
The Amish shun publicity but they can be visited in their communities in Ohio and Pennsylvania.

Jon Cutrell, 22622 SR 119, Goshen, Indianapolis 46526, USA. Mennonite quilter.

Stanley Kaufman, Kaufman Gallery, Box 185, Berlin, Ohio 44610, USA. Amish and Mennonite art gallery. Pages 17-19.

Lancaster Towne Quilts, Box 277, Strasburg, PA 17579, USA (717-687-8600)

Museum Quilts, 3rd Floor, 254-258 Goswell Road, London EC1V 7EB (0171-490 7732). Page 12.

The American Quilters' Society, PO Box 3290, Paducah, KY 42001, USA

The National Quilting Association, PO Box 393, Ellicott City, MD 21043-0393, USA

The People's Place, Amish Museum, Main Street, Intercourse, PA 17534, USA

TRADITIONAL SAMPLERS
Joanne Harvey, PO Box 2554, Dearborn, Michigan 48123, USA. Traditional and reproduction samplers. Pages 25-27.

Caroline Vincent, Little Cott, Burton Common, Petworth, Sussex (01798 7328)

The American Sewing Guild, PO Box 50976, Indianapolis, IN 46250-0976, USA

RAG RUGS
Louisa Creed, 27 Norfolk Street, York YO2 1JY. Rag rugs.

Lizzie Reakes, 68 Oaklands Road, Hanwell, Ealing, London W7 2DU (0181-840 7579). Hand-tufted and rag rugs.

Jenni Stuart-Anderson, The Birches, Middleton-on-the-Hill, Herefordshire HR5 0HZ (01568 750229). Hooked and plaited rag rugs and wallhangings. Page 28.

Emma Tennant, Shaws, Newcastleton, Roxburghshire TD9 0SH. Rag rugs. Pages 32-35.

Joan Yeomans, Oakfield Lodge, Poyston Cross, Haverfordwest, Pembrokeshire SA62 4EB (01437 766159). Rag rugs.

FELTWORK
Sarah Barker, Unit 3B, King Street Mews, King Street, London N2 8DY (0181-442 0590). Fleece slippers. Page 36 below.

Clare Beaton, 15 Kelross, London N5 2QS. Felt hats, garments and accessories. Pages 39-41.

Heather Belcher, 39 Casella Road, London SE14 5QN

Lene Nielson, 76 Main Gate, Hepworth, West Yorkshire HD7 1TJ. Feltwork.

Jean Rudland, Flat 1, Datchet House, Church Road, Brettenham, Ipswich, Suffolk IP7 7QR (01449 736068). Hand-dyed felt pictures. Page 38 below right.

Christina Sargent, Wheems, Eastside, South Ronaldsay, Orkney KW17 2JT (01856 831537). Hand-felted rugs and wall hangings, naturally coloured, home-dyed local fleeces.

Vicky Sheard, 365 Oakleigh Road North, Whetstone, London N20 0RJ (0181-368 8942). Felt wall hangings.

KITCHENCRAFT

BASKETS
Lois Walpole, Rapid Eye Baskets, 100 Fairfoot Road, London E3 4EH (0171-538 5308). Baskets from recycled materials. Pages 48-51.

FLOORCLOTHS
Bery Designs, 157 St Johns Hill, London SW11 1PQ (0171-924 2197).

Susan Carter Keffury, PO Box 8165, Berkeley, California 94707 (510-524-3214). Painted floorcloths. Page 52 top right, 53 bottom right.

Philadelphia Floorcloths Inc., 510 Merwyn Road, Narbeth, Pennsylvania 19072, USA

Christine Smith, 110 Graham Way, Devon, PA 19333, USA. American folk-art floorcloths. Pages 56-59.

Natalie Woolf, 10 Wharfdale Street, Leeds, West Yorkshire (0113 2422297). Painted floorcloths. Pages 52 top left, 53 bottom left.

CHIMNEY BOARDS
Belinda Ballantine, The Old Dairy, Pinkney Park, Malmesbury, Wiltshire SN16 0NY (01666 841144). Decoupage screens, clocks and painted furniture.

Darrell Gardner, 13 Swinfield Road, Whitstable, Kent CT35 4HL. Painted screens, chimney boards and trays.

PUNCHED TIN
James Palotas, HC31, Box 321, Williamsport, PA 17701, USA (717-478-2010). Pages 72-75.

WOODCRAFT

SHAKER AND AMISH WOODWORK
C.H. Becksvoort, Box 12, New Gloucester, Maine 04260, USA (207-926-4608). Furniture maker, weathervanes and restoration work for the Shakers.

Tony Butler, Unit J, Pentre Wen, Gobowen, Oswestry, Shropshire SY10 7JZ (01691 670425). Shaker boxes, trays and stools.

Moira Hankinson, Somerset Creative Projects, Laurel Farm, Westham, Wedmoor, Somerset BS28 4UZ (01934 712416). Somerset trugs, distress-painted interior and garden accessories and furniture by mail order. Pages 82-87.

WOODEN TOYS
Nicola Henshaw, 40½ Workshops, 40½ Wandsworth Road, London SW8 2JP (0171 627 8747). Wooden animals. Pages 92-97.

Margaret Oakshett, The Lodge, Christchurch Road, Cheltenham GL50 2RV. Wooden animals.

WEATHERVANES
Ivan Barnett, RDI, Stevens, Pennsylvania 17578, USA

J. Donald Felix, PO Box 995, Hampton, New Hampshire 03842, USA. (603-474-2225). Weathervanes.

Chris Mowe, The Pine Brush/ Colourman, Coton Clanford, Stafford ST18 9PB (01785 282799). Reproduction paints and specialist brushes by mail order; weathervanes to commission. Pages 104-107.

GAMEBOARDS
Fiona Denholm, Tullygunn, Camp Road, Comrie, Perthshire PH6 2HA (01764 670877). Gameboards. Page 109.

Sue Martin, RD 3, Box 119, Red Hook, New York 12571, USA. Gameboards. Pages 112-115.

AUTOMATA
John Maltby, The Orchard House, Stoneshill, Crediton, Devon EX17 4EF (01363 772753). Automata and ceramics. Pages 120-123.

Tony Mann, Goodcott, Ashreicgney, Chulmleigh, Devon EX18 7NE (01769 520 284). Automata.

Peter Markey, Gellidywyll, Bontdolgadfan, Llanbrynmair, Powys SY19 7AP (01650 521539). Automata.

Opi Toys, Trewoon Cottage, Nancledra, Penzance, Cornwall TR20 8NB (01736 740421). Automata.

ANIMAL HOUSES
Bob and Charlotte Lanier, Big Bear on Cosby, 777 Bear Road, Cosby, TN 37722, USA (615-487-3320). Birdhouses. Pages 128-131.

Mette Farmer, Dolittle Designs, Chaucer House, Bawdeswell, Dereham, Norfolk NR20 4RT (01362 688 578). Animal houses. Page 124.

DECORATIVE CRAFT

PAINTED CERAMICS
Julie Arnall, 12B Linden Gardens, London W2 4ES (0171-221 0180). Decorated handmade porcelain vessels, tiles and tableware.

Elizabeth Evans, 17 Cornwall Terrace, Penzance, Cornwall (01736 330565). Painted ceramics.

Paul Jackson, Helland Bridge Pottery, Helland Bridge, Bodmin. Hand-thrown, hand-painted and sprayed under-glaze colours.

Anne Laycock, Holmes Grange Craft Centre, Heathlands Road, Wokingham, Berks RG11 3AW. Designer and decorative painter.

Mike Levy, 6 Victoria Street, Brighton BN1 3FP (01273 327870)

Richard Lowther, Chemin du Vallon. Equemauville, 14600 Honfleur, France (33-31-89-44-41). Painted pots. Pages 137-143.

LAMPSHADES
Caroline Ashworth Lampshades, W.K. Howarth, Unit 1 A&B Blyth Road, Industrial Estate, Halesworth, Suffolk IP19 8EN (01986 4417)

Cressida Bell, 1a Princeton Street, London WC1R 4AX (0171 404 3191). Page 144.

Susie Clayton, PO Box 78, Twickenham TW1 1EV (0181 892 2300)

Andrea Maflin, 50 Crofton Road, London NW5 1EN (0171 284 1224). Lampshades. Pages 147-151.

PAPIER MÂCHÉ
Madeleine Adams, Cobweb, Stourton Hill, Warwickshire CV36 5HE. Papier Mâché. Page 153.

Gerry Copp, School Cottage, Ainthorpe, Lincoln LN1 2SG (01522 730218)

Marion Elliot, 91 Huddleston Road, Tufnell Park, London N7 0AE (0171 607 9402)

Margaret Frere-Smith, Whitehouse Farmhouse, Uggeshall, Nr Beccles, Suffolk. Page 154.

Sarah Kelly, 70 Squires Bridge Road, Shepperton, Middlesex TW17 0QA (01932 564557). Papier Mâché.

Yanina Temple, 15 York Road, Loughborough, Leicestershire LE11 2DA (01509 218160)

FLOTSAM AND JETSAM
Joan Molloy, Sterts Centre, Upton Cross, Liskeard, Cornwall PL14 5AZ (01579 362962). Clocks. Pages 165-169.

Louise Slater, 205 Wandsworth Workshops, 86-96 Garratt Lane, London SW18 4DJ (0181 8706761)

Victor Stuart Graham, 73 Montpelier Road, Brighton BN1 3BD. Driftwood boats. Pages 162-163.

Karen Tanç, Ground Floor Flat, Albemarle Mansions, Medina Terrace, Hove, Sussex. Driftwood mirrors. Pages 162-163.

BOOKBINDING
Compton Marbling, Lower Lawn Barns, Tisbury, Salisbury, Wilts SP3 6SG. Page 172 right.

Downside Abbey Bindery, Abbey Road, Stratton-on-the-Fosse, Nr Bath BA3 4QW (01761 233392)

Rob Shepherd Bookbinders Ltd, 76 Rochester Row, London SW1P 1JU (0171 630 1184). Pages 173-177.

Undercover, 70 Wilna Road, London SW18 3BA (0181 871 2529)

PAINTED FURNITURE
John Anderson, 20 Silvergate, Blickling, Norwich NR11 6NN (01263 735270)

Cressida Bell, 1a Princeton Street, London WC1R 4AX (0171 404 3191). Painted furniture and textiles. Pages 185-187.

Somerset Country Furniture, 632 Fulham Road, London SW6 5RJ (0171 371 0436)

GENERAL CRAFTS
Appalachia, 14A George Street, St Albans, Herts AL3 4ER (01727 836796). American folk-art.

Christopher Gurshin, Box 616, Newburyport, Massachusetts 09150, USA. Rural paintings and tin-ware.

Julie Hagan Bloch, 51 Mongaup Road, Hurleyville, New York, NY 12747, USA. Rubber-stamps.

George Thomson, The White Cottage, Balgrie Bank, Bonny Bank, Leven, Fife KY8 5SL. Rubber-stamps.

CRAFT ORGANIZATIONS

Crafts Council, 44A Pentonville Road, Islington, London N1 9BY, (0171-278 7700)

London Arts Board, Elme House, 133 Long Acre, London WC2E 9AF, (0171-240 1313)

South East Arts, 10 Mount Ephraim, Tunbridge Wells TN4 8AS, (01892 515210)

Southern Arts, 13 St Clement Street, Winchester SO23 9DQ, (01962 855099)

South West Arts, Bradninch Place, Gandy Street, Exeter EX4 3LS, (01392 218188)

Eastern Arts, Cherry Hinton Hall, Cambridge CB1 4DW, (01223 215355)

East Midlands Arts, Mountfields House, Epinal Way, Loughborough LE11 OQE, (0509 218292)

West Midlands Arts, 82 Granville Street, Birmingham B1 2LH, (021-631 3121)

Arts Board North West, Manchester House, 22 Bridge Street, Manchester M3 3AB, (0161-834 6644)

Yorkshire and Humberside Arts, 21 Bond Street, Dewsbury WF13 1AX, (01924 455555)

Northern Arts, 10 Osborne Terrace, Newcastle-upon-Tyne NE2 1NZ, (0191-281 6334)

The Scottish Arts Council, 12 Manor Place, Edinburgh EH3 7DD, (0131-226 6051)

Wales Craft Council, Park Lane House, 7 High Street, Welshpool, Powys SY21 7SP, (01938 555313)

BIBLIOGRAPHY

Andrew, H. E. Laye, *The Batsford Encyclopedia of Crafts*, Batsford; Bawden, J., *The Art and Craft of Papier Mâché*, Mitchell Beazley; Beaton, Clare, *The Felt Book*, Collins & Brown; Bishop, Dr Robert, *American Folk Art*, Museum of American Folk Art; Caulfield, S. F. A. and Saward, B. C., *The Dictionary of Needlework*, Blaketon Hall; Clabburn, P., *Samplers*, Shire Publications; The Diagram Group, *The Way to Play*, Corgi; Flick, P., *Discovering Toys and Toy Museums*, Shire Publications; Garden City Publishing Co., *The Practical Book of American Antiques*; Gostelow, M., *Embroidery*, Cavendish House; Graham, C., *Dummy Boards and Chimney Boards*, Shire Publications; Hansell, P. and J., *Dovecotes*, Shire Publications; Hodges, F., *Period Pastimes*, Weidenfeld and Nicolson; Hodges, H., *Pottery*, Hamlyn; Hollander, A., *Bookcraft*, Van Nostrand Reinhold; Innes, Jocasta, *Scandinavian Painted Decor*, Cassell; Jackson, Valerie, *Crafts*, Lutterworth Press; Jenkins, Susan and Seward, Linda, *Quilts: The American Story*, Harper Collins; Kauffman, Henry L., *Pennsylvania Dutch American Folk Art*, Dover; King, Constance, *Metal Toys and Automata*, The Apple Press; King, Eileen, *Toys and Dolls for Collectors*, Hamlyn; Knopf, A., *The Knopf Collectors' Guides to American Antiques: Folk Art*; Krueger, Glee, *New England Samplers to 1840*, Old Sturbridge Village; Linsley, Leslie, *Hooked Rugs. An American Folk Art*, Clarkson Potter; Lipman, J., *American Folk Art in Wood, Metal and Stone*, Dover; Lipman, J., *Techniques in American Folk Decoration*, Dover; Love, Brian, *Play the Game*, Michael Joseph and Ebury Press; McCauley, K., *Decorative Arts of the Amish of Lancaster County*, Good Books; Morley-Fletcher, H., *Ceramics*, Tiger; Nichol, J., *the Complete Guide to Pet Care*, Christopher Helm; Niles, Bo, *Country Living Country Decorating*, Hearst Books; Paine, S., *Embroidered Textiles*, Thames & Hudson; Riley, N., *Tile Art*, The Apple Press; Sears, M. Seehafer, *Country Look*, Ebury Press; Spilhaus, A. and K., *Mechanical Toys*, Robert Hale; Sprigg, J., *Shaker Design*, Whitney Norton; Stapleton, C., *Crafts of America*, Harper and Row; Tennant, E., *Rag Rugs of England and America*, Walker Books; Wilson, P., *The Victoria & Albert Museum*, Scala; Wiseman, E. J., *Victorian Do-it-Yourself*, David & Charles.

AUTHOR'S ACKNOWLEDGEMENTS

I would like to thank all the contributors for the time, patience and enthusiasm which have gone into each of their craft projects. I would like to acknowledge the particular help of Joan Osofsky, for advice on American crafts. Susan Jenkins for her help with quiltmakers. Chris Farr for supplying his rug. Vivien Hicks for lending us her Amish dolls. George Thomson for his endpaper design. Karen Tanc for making up her driftwood mirrors. John Maltby, Emma Tennant and Nick and Moira Hankinson for allowing their work to be transported back and forwards. Charlotte and Bob Lanier for their kindness and hospitality and Stanley Kaufman for sharing his knowledge of Amish and Mennonite art. I would also like to thank the team at Conran Octopus – Louise, Alison, Mary and Jane – whose enthusiasm, humour, impeccable taste and serene tolerance was enough to make writing in an office bearable. Lucy and Clay took some classic photographs, which Julia patiently supplemented. Finally, Deirdre McSharry and my sisters Jocasta and Judy – all guiding lights when it comes to the practicalities and the pleasures of paper, paint and prose.

PICTURE CREDITS

The publishers wish to thank the following photographers and organizations for their kind permission to reproduce the following images:
4 J. P. Godeaut; 5 above left Emma Tennant; 5 above right & below left Michael Freeman; 5 below right IPC Magazines/Robert Harding Syndication; 6 right Yves Duronsoy; 8 IPC Magazines/Robert Harding Syndication; 12 Museum Quilts Publications; 13 Mel Horst; 14 Michael Freeman; 15 Mel Horst; 20 IPC Magazines/Robert Harding Syndication; 21 David Parmiter; 22 Marie Claire Idées/C. Fleurent, P. Chastres; 24 Elizabeth Whiting & Associates/Neil Lorimer; 28 Jenni Stuart-Anderson; 29 Tiggy Ruthven; 30 © image Dennis Krukowski/*The Farmhouse*, Bantam; 31 above right Mel Horst; 31 below Shelburne Museum, Shelburne, Vermont, photo by Ken Burris; 36 below Sarah Barker; 37 The World of Interiors/Fritz von Der Schulenburg; 38 above Ian Skelton/Heather Belcher; 38 below right Jean Rudland; 42 Michael Freeman; 42–3 IPC Magazines/Robert Harding Syndication; 44 right & 45 IPC Magazines/Robert Harding Syndication; 46 above left Explorer; 46 below Michael Freeman; 47 Paul Ryan; 52 Susan Carter-Keffury; 53 above left Natalie Woolf; 53 above right Susan Carter-Keffury; 53 below left Natalie Woolf, 53 below right Susan Carter-Keffury; 54 Elizabeth Whiting & Associates/Rodney Hyatt; 55 Bery Designs; Anna Nockholds 60; Susie Wilkinson/Alex Ramsay 61; John Bouchier 63; 68 above left David Downie; 68 below right Stylograph/John Hall; 69–71 Camera Press Ltd; 71 right IPC Magazines/Robert Harding Syndication; 76 Michael Freeman; 76–7 Lucy Mason; 78 top left & top right Michael Freeman; 79 Michael Freeman; 80 Walter Smalling Jr; 81 Philadelphia Museum of Art: The Titus Geesy Collection, Craftsman's Handbook by Henry Lapp; 88 above J. P. Godeaut; 88 below Michael Freeman; 89 Arcaid/Lucinda Lambton; 90 left Michael Freeman; 90 right Yves Duronsoy; 91 above left Yves Duronsoy; 91 above Michael Freeman; 91 below right Christian Sarramon; 98 below Shelburne Museum, Shelburne, Vermont, photo by Ken Burris; 98 above right Appalachia; 99 © image/Dennis Krukowski/Nancy Frierberg Antiques, USA; 100 Arcaid/Richard Bryant; 101 Marie Claire Maison/Cristophe Dugied; 108 Appalachia; 109 Fiona Denholm; 110 above left Sara Delafield Cook/Carl Little; below left Fiona Denholm; right Arcaid/Richard Bryant; 111 right Walter Smalling; 116 S. Dutton/Edessia Aghajanian; 118 above right Edessia Aghajanian/Private Collection; 117 Arcaid/Julie Phipps; 118 centre Edessia Aghajanian; 119 Michael Freeman; 124 left Rex Features; 124 right Gary Rogers; 126 Marijke Heuff, Brinkworth; 125 Arcaid/Lucinda Lambton; 132 IPC Magazines/Robert Harding Syndication; 132–3 Yves Duronsoy, A. M Ollier (potter); 134–5 Marie Claire Idées/G. Chabaneix, C. Chabaneix; 136/Michael Boys/Boys Syndication; 145 Suzie Clayton; 146 Marie Clare Maison/J. P. Verger, B. Jacquelin; 152 above left Marie Claire Maison/G Chabaneix, D. Rozenstrach; 152 below right Jacqui Hurst; 153 Madeleine Adams; 154 Margaret Frere-Smith; 155–6 Marie Claire Maison/Maltaverne/Faven; 160 Michael Freeman; 161 Camera Press; 164 Marie Claire Maison/Hussenot/Comte; 172 right Elle Decoration/Hugh Johnson, stylist Barbara Hajek, courtesy Undercover; 172 left Compton Marbling; 170 IPC Magazines/Robert Harding Syndication; 171 Camera Press Ltd; 178 Marie Claire Maison above/Fleurant, Chastres; 178 below centre & right Somerset Country; 179 Boys Syndication; 180 Jessie Walker; 181 Yves Duronsoy; 182 Guy Bouchet; 183 Paul Ryan/International Interiors.
The following photographs were specially taken for Conran Octopus by Lucy Mason: 3, 6 left, 7, 32–5, 36 above, 39, 40–1, 44, 48–9, 50–1, 64–7, 84–5, 82–7, 92–5, 96–7, 102–7, 120–1, 122–3, 137–143, 147–151, 157–9, 162–3, 165–9, 173–7, 184–7. The following photographs were specially taken for Conran Octopus by Clay Perry: 2, 9, 10, 16, 17, 18, 19, 25, 26, 56, 57, 58, 72, 73, 74, 75, 112, 113, 114, 115, 127, 128, 129, 130, 131.
Photographs on pp. 1 & 44 by Ultrachrome.

INDEX

Page numbers in **bold** refer to the illustrations